The End
of Suffering

The End
of Suffering

Joseph F. Girzone

ORBIS BOOKS
Maryknoll, New York 10545

Published by Orbis Books, Maryknoll, New York 10545–0302.
Manufactured in the United States of America.
Copy editing and typesetting by Joan Weber Laflamme.

Library of Congress Cataloging-in-Publication Data

Girzone, Joseph F.
    The end of suffering / Joseph F. Girzone.
        pages cm
        ISBN 978–1–62698–025–9 (pbk.)
        1. Suffering—Religious aspects—Christianity. I. Title.
    BV4909.G58 2013
231'.8—dc23

                                            2012049848

Contents

ભ

Contents

Acknowledgments

വ

Deacon Gary Riggi, is formator of the diaconate program for the Catholic Diocese of Albany, New York, and who works with me in The Joshua Foundation, was the motivating force behind the subject of this book, so he deserves great credit if this work touches people's lives. I do admit it was not an easy book to write; it took almost three years to finish. Even when I completed it, I was not totally satisfied, so I sent it to my friend and editor Michael Leach with hope and trepidation. Having just finished reading his editing of the manuscript, I am amazed at how masterly he has woven everything together into a beautifully polished work. And I would like to thank Mike's wonderful wife, Vickie, for supporting him in his important work that helps so many people. And again, thank you, Ponie Sheehan, for the stunning art work on the cover, which radiates the joy and hope that can mystically come from suffering. And for the fourth time with my books the production department of Orbis Books has produced a class work.

Preface

CR

One day a little lamb rang the doorbell of the rectory where I was living. The housekeeper answered the door and saw a frightened child, a girl of about twelve. "Can I help you, young lady?"

"Yes, ma'am. Does Priest live here?"

"Yes."

"Can I see Priest?"

"Of course, come right in and sit down, and I will get the priest."

When I entered the office, I was surprised to see such a worried child. "Hello, young lady."

"Are you Priest?"

"Yes, what can I do to help you?"

With trembling lips, she told me, "Priest, I was going to have a baby, and my mother was very upset. She made me get into the car and brought me to the doctor's office. The doctor brought me into another room and told me to take my clothes off and get up on a bench with a mattress on it. He then gave me some kind of medicine, and I began to get sleepy. Then he opened my legs and started to do something to me, but I was very sleepy, so I don't know what he did. When I woke up, he took me out to my mother. On the way home, my mother said to me, 'Well, we don't have to worry about you having that baby anymore.'

"When she said that I felt as if something horrible had been done to me, and I got even more scared. I started to cry, and my mother got upset and told me not to tell anybody what happened. When I went to bed, I couldn't sleep. I felt I was bad, that I'd done something evil, and that God was angry and didn't love me anymore. I was afraid to talk to him. Can you help me, Priest?"

My heart felt broken, too. "Little one, you didn't do anything wrong. What people did to you was wrong, but you are a beautiful and innocent young lady, and God loves you very much. So, don't feel bad. God feels sorry for what people have done to you, and he will protect you no matter what anyone might say, so don't worry."

"You mean I'm not evil?"

"No, you are good. You are God's perfect child. You're an innocent young girl, so don't be afraid to talk to God and feel his love. He will always love you no matter what."

Her whole being seemed to relax, and she smiled. "That makes me so happy, Priest. Can I hug you?"

I got down on one knee, and she threw her arms around me and we hugged. She kissed me on the cheek and said, "Thank you so much. I am happy now." Then she turned to walk toward the door. I let her out and watched as she walked up the street and started to skip.

I didn't know the girl or what religion she belonged to, or even what her name was. I could tell she wasn't familiar with priests. I don't know what happened to her after she left because I never saw her again.

All I could think of is that, in some way, Jesus the Good Shepherd knew that little girl could be scarred emotionally, psychologically, and spiritually for the rest of her life and found a way to protect her. I think often about the Good Shepherd, who no longer is limited to the villages and towns of Palestine but has as his flock all human beings, no matter what their place or race, their color or nationality, their religion. He has the same concern for the suffering of all his sheep today as he did then, and as the Good Shepherd he now wanders the world day and night endlessly seeking out the sheep in whatever perilous places he finds them. He gently reaches out to them, even though they may not know him, and comforts and consoles them with his healing love.

We are all, each of us, that little girl. No matter who we are—president, pope, king, queen, head of state, or just an ordinary person—we all have times when we burn inside or suffer from physical pain. Many of us try to keep it to ourselves, but often that isn't healthy, especially if we do not have the skills to process what we are experiencing. Emotional pain is particularly difficult. Betrayal by a dear friend cuts deeply, and the loss of one or more loved ones at the same time has no ready explanation. Natural disasters and terrorist attacks create such havoc that they make us wonder where the loving, benevolent God is during all these happenings, or even if he exists.

As difficult as suffering is for us to understand, this little book is a modest endeavor to approach this impossible phenomenon in a way that helps us see at least some beneficial and positive purposes to our suffering. And to know that we, too, are God's perfect children; no matter what, we are all right; and that all will somehow be well.

1

What Is Suffering?

Suffering, or pain, is an unpleasant feeling caused by an emotional, psychological, or physical experience that disturbs our well-being and our peace of mind, and causes great discomfort. The first pain in my life that I remember was psychological. I was a little more than a year old. My father had a German Shepherd that he loved but that frightened my mother. I could hear my father and mother arguing about the dog. One night while they were quarrelling, my father stormed out of the house with the dog, and I became afraid and could not sleep.

I kept standing up in my crib, thinking that I was asking my mother (though I really couldn't talk yet), "Is Daddy coming home?" She mumbled something through her tears, but it did not comfort me. I still had a terrible feeling that I did not like. Was it fear? Was it anxiety? Whatever it was, all I knew was that it was dreadful. I could not sleep for a long time and then finally drifted off. When I woke up the next morning, my mother said something to me. Whatever it was made me sense that my father had come home and later left for work. And there was no dog. I felt better. But that whole awful incident was traumatic. I never forgot it, and even today, eighty years later, just to think of it affects me.

Looking back on that night and the effect it had on me made me realize in some small way the terrible damage done to so many little children who suffer the horribly painful experiences of parents fighting all throughout their tender years. For them, that is normal. I can understand how in some cases it is nearly impossible for the victims of such experiences to deal with life and with people in a normal and healthy way when they grow older. After endless years of counseling troubled people, I have learned that the experiences of meanness and hate, and very often physical violence for many children, is little different from the training of attack animals, and I can understand why some criminals act the way they do. They were trained from their most innocent, tender years to trust no one, to be suspicious of everyone, and to hate, since that was all they knew from infancy. They never learned what it was like to love or to be loved. Their parents or guardians may not have intended to teach them to hate or to practice criminal behavior, but what their children were exposed to was little different from the training of vicious animals.

Having been trained that way, how could the children act any differently? And when they act out, they are immediately arrested as cold-blooded, hardened criminals deserving of the worst punishments, when they themselves had been pitiful victims since infancy. Only understanding, compassion and love have any hope of healing their damaged souls. But society rarely has the compassion for that. We are too much into retribution and punishment, and we approve the sadistic administering of justice.

My next experience of pain was emotional. The first creature I met who was small like me became my friend. He was a little boy who lived next door. A short time later he moved away, and I could not understand why. He was my friend, yet I would never see him again. Why? That hurt, a new kind of hurt. I had lost someone I liked.

My next experience of pain came shortly later. When I was four years old I walked down to the corner store one day and saw a girl talking to some friends as they were walking home from school. She was much older than I, and she was beautiful. I immediately fell in love with her and walked down to the corner store every school day to see her. I know she never noticed me; she was probably in sixth or seventh grade. Every day I would see her and just look at how beautiful she was. I wished she would just notice me, but she didn't even know I existed. Then one day I heard her saying goodbye to her friends. She was moving. They all said goodbye and hugged her. She got on the bus and left my life forever. I was devastated. When I went back home, I sat on the front steps and nursed my broken heart. No one knew the pain I was suffering. I always kept my pain to myself. That was the worst pain I had experienced so far. It was terrible. Would the pain ever go away? That too was emotional pain, a terrible pain of loss. It took me the longest time to forget that beautiful creature. Her name was Thelma Steubert. After all these years her image is still fresh in my memory.

But one day I was to experience something that tore me apart. When it was happening, I thought I was going to die. Some other children, older than I, grabbed me and threw me down on the ground. Two of them held my eyes open while another poured fine gravel into my eyes. I screamed in agony, and I thought I was never going to see again. Then they let me go. I couldn't open my eyes; they were both bleeding profusely. I finally found my way home, which was not very far away. When I went into the house, my mother almost went out of her mind when she saw the blood flowing out of my eyes.

She then helped me to lie down on the floor. She made a weak solution of boric acid and, with balls of cotton, gently let the solution drip slowly into my eyes, one drop at a time. She was so careful. It took the longest time. Finally, with patience, she was able to remove every small piece of gravel from my eyes. Then she brought me into the bedroom, had me lie down on the bed, and told me to try to sleep and let my eyes rest. We both prayed hard that God would not let me go blind and that my eyes would get better.

My eyes burned for the longest time, it seemed like weeks, but it was only for a few days. Thank God I could see again, as the pain and soreness gradually went away. That experience was a horrible shock in so many ways. Those children had been my friends, and I felt betrayed. I forget who they were; all I remember is that they were play-mates. I had never experienced meanness before, and this kind of pain was complicated because it was not just physical, but mental, emotional, and psychological, involving an array of emotions—fear, anxiety, anger, desperation, hope. After all the years that have passed, the memory is still vivid. As a child though, it is amazing how resilient I was. It took just a little time to get past what had happened and get on with the adventure of enjoying each new experience. Every day was filled with fun and surprises, because everything in life at that age is for the first time, and even little things are filled with wonder.

An important part of my childhood was loneliness. I didn't know then what loneliness was, but I seemed always alone, and I felt a certain sadness, a tranquil kind of sadness. Maybe I was afraid of being hurt. I guess it was partially because I was afraid to trust people because of things that happened. I was learning that people could be mean. Other experiences reinforced that fear. One day as I was walking down to the corner store to buy some candy, a group of older boys were hanging around the corner. They always made fun of me because I was Italian. This particular day they took the cover off the sewer drain in the street and put me in the sewer and put the cover back on and left me there. I was panicky. I don't remember crying or screaming or anything. I cannot imagine not reacting in some way. Eventually someone did come over and lift me out. I think it was one of the nicer boys in the group that had put me in there. I was maybe eight or nine at the time.

Loneliness became my constant companion. It made me create my own little world where I could live peacefully, a world of make believe. I loved baseball and followed all the games on the radio. I kept records of all my baseball heroes, with their averages, and went to Hawkins Stadium to watch the Albany Senators when they were home for the games. My biggest thrill was the night I saw Babe Ruth play at an exposition game. Of course, I went by myself. I never realized until lately how much I was alone as a child, but I enjoyed my peaceful world. I learned to draw and paint, and painted a lot of pictures, particularly of sunsets and of old farm houses out in the country, usually winter scenes with snow covering a house and the surrounding fields. I guess even the pictures projected a lonely feeling.

I never looked upon the loneliness as suffering, though; it was just the way I was. It was like a quiet sadness, living in a world of my mind where there were only pleasant fantasies. My brothers and sisters were real and were a happy part of my life, but my life's adventures were in another world that was inside of me. I think perhaps that may have been the reason why I was so attracted to daily mass once I made my first communion. I believed Jesus was real and his presence in communion was real, and he became my friend. It was real. His friendship was real. When I was hurting, I talked to my friend, and I felt better. I never shared with anyone else.

When my grandmother died, I was in the third grade. That was a very difficult time, and I was sad. She was my friend. I used to go to her apartment next door and visit her when she was very ill. She was comforted when I put a washcloth with cold water on her forehead. It made her happy. Then one day she died. I did not know what death was, and when my mother explained it, I still did not understand. Watching the men carry her coffin to the hearse and take her away was terrible, knowing I would never see her again. That was so painful. It was at times like that that my friend Jesus was my comfort, and his nearness brought peace to my troubled soul.

It's strange when I look back on those days. I wonder how I discovered I could have Jesus for a friend. Was I searching for him, or was he searching for me? When I found him as a child he immediately became real, and it took no time at all to find that his presence was healing. That part was not fantasy. That part was real. He was there. Maybe my loneliness was preparing me for that. That relationship became my religion, and I was grateful to the church for bringing him to me, especially in communion. When I was hurting most, having him come into my soul made everything all right. It was like he was holding my soul in his arms, and I felt at peace.

I cannot understand the thinking of some writers today who refer to Jesus as the supreme example of human potential and the model for each of us to develop the consciousness of our own divinity, and that the divinity he attained by his life brought him to the level of other gods like Buddha. I don't think these authors are aware of the reality of Jesus' transcendence throughout the universe. It makes me wonder what their definition of God is. Is a god just a human who developed to a higher degree than others whatever potential for greatness supposedly exists within each of us? If there is a God he didn't *become* a god. He is God from eternity, with omnipotence and omniscience, all powerful and all knowing. There can only be one being who is all powerful and to whom all else is subject. And this God is not a static model. He is a dynamic presence that transcends all being. So, when I was close to Jesus as a child, I knew he was present with me and it was not make believe. He was really my friend, with me constantly. When we experience such a vivid reality, we will never again see Jesus as a mere lifeless model. And when Jesus shares his own insights with us, we know we did not just dream them up.

That friendship with Jesus did strange things to me. It separated me, not from reality, but from an attachment to things and to the world around me, and made his world real to me. Part of Jesus' world was saints, people who fell in love with Jesus. I felt drawn to them in a powerful way. I found that there were books about saints and stores where I could buy them. The saints, too, became my friends. They were willing to undertake the most courageous ventures to show their love for Jesus. I wanted to be like them. One of my heroes was Damien of Molokai, a Belgian priest who went to work among the lepers in the South Pacific. He eventually died while caring for those unfortunate people, himself a victim of leprosy. As a young boy I wanted to do the same thing, give my life to God, and go to Molokai to work with the lepers.

That world was where I found peace and a wonderful feeling of joy. It was as if I had become a stranger to the world I lived in. That world seemed real, but Jesus' friendship and my friendship with the saints were more real. It was not that I had a break with reality. There were still areas of the material world around me where I found meaning and excitement. One part of the world I did enjoy was school. I liked to learn new things and could get lost in reading about people in other countries and about life in the early colonies. I did well in school, and from the first day, and for the next eight years, I sat next to a girl named Irene Morini, who had become my friend, though we hardly ever saw each other outside school. I found it hard being close to anyone. I suppose I was afraid of being hurt. When we reached the seventh and eighth grade, Irene was popular with other boys, and I just looked on from a distance, hurting inside, resigning myself to believe that she had wandered off into another world in which I never felt comfortable. Knowing I intended to go into the seminary soon, though I hadn't told my parents, there was nothing I could do if Irene was interested in other boys. By that time I was involved in sports, and I played football or baseball practically every day after school. I was popular with my baseball team because I was fast, could pitch fast, and was a good batter; I was a good quarterback when we played football, never, of course, with uniforms or shoulder pads or helmets. The rougher the better, the more fun it was, even though we went limping home afterward from charley horses and battered muscles.

My childhood really ended when I told my parents after my graduation that I wanted to enter the seminary. They registered no surprise; they were aware that I had sent for a booklet from the Carmelite seminary in Middletown, New York. They asked if I wanted to leave home at such a young age. I told them I was ready and in my mind had been planning for it for over a year.

When I left, I was no longer a child. Life away from home opened my eyes to a whole new world. Childhood suddenly ended. Everything was now structured and efficiently regimented. The child world was no more. This new world was exciting, and I threw myself into it with gusto. The loneliness of my early years, though a type of suffering, was the climate that ushered me into life in another world, the world of the spirit, which became an exciting journey and my life's adventure. Later I could see even more clearly that the solitude born of loneliness can be the fertile soil of creative talent.

With my life now on a new path, my introduction to the childhood difficulties ended, and the new life promised to be the beginning of a thrilling adventure. Although I did not understand it at the time, all those childhood experiences were part of a lifelong training program for the future. One permanent effect they had on me was to open my inner life to Jesus at a very young age. He was the one person, other than my mother and father, whom I could trust as a friend. Now, seventy years later, I can look back and see that God was never removed from my life; nor was anything that happened irrelevant to the meaning of my future. I learned that I was not unique. God has the same caring involvement in the lives of each of us, showing vividly, even if it is not obvious at each moment, that the Good Shepherd is still very much the watchful guardian of our well-being and our personal destiny. This learning would be the lighthouse that helped me see and care about the suffering of others.

2

Suffering in Childhood

Children's pain came into focus early in my life as a priest, not only from reflecting on my own experiences, but also as I grew older and became acquainted with so many children who had difficult lives. The memory of the unpleasant experience of my parents' angry words over my father having a German Shepherd, and the terrible effect it had on me emotionally, made me think of children who experience not just one incident but daily and nightly experiences, which for them is often the norm. I started to wonder what happens to them emotionally and psychologically if they are subjected to this kind of trauma over a long period of time, especially if it involves frequent violent behavior as well.

When I was first teaching school in the Bronx after my ordination, a number of the students were from troubled homes. I could tell which ones by the way they behaved in school. Some days several of them seemed to have not slept all night; they were irritable, and it took little for them to flare up. They seemed distracted, unable to concentrate, as if they were having troubling thoughts—and the problem was not girls. These were hurting beings. In getting to know them, I found that many had nervous stomachs, as if they were developing ulcers, due to constant stress at home. But I also noticed that they were much more open to affection and friendship, as if they were starving for them. When they became a friend, they clung, a friend for life. These older boys and girls were reflecting the effects of their earlier experiences, which were now showing in their adolescent personalities.

One boy told me he was sorry for acting up in class. When I mentioned to him that I understood, that I knew he was hurting, he got tears in his eyes and told me he had no father and that his mother worked nights and he rarely saw her. He hated going home to an empty apartment. He felt like an orphan.

He was just one among many. I ended up becoming their shepherd, and for many of them, a father figure; they as much as told me so.

Later, when I was assigned to a high school in Pottsville, Pennsylvania, I was driving along a street in a nice neighborhood when I spotted a young boy peeking into people's living room windows. It was Thanksgiving afternoon. I stopped the car a little farther away from the house so as not to surprise the boy, slowly walked along the sidewalk, and quietly said, "Does it look nice in there, sonny?" I had my Roman collar on, and he could see I was a priest.

"Yes, that's a nice house. They have a nice family. I'm not doing anything bad, Father. I just wanted to see what it's like to have a family on Thanksgiving."

"Don't you have a family?"

"No, I'm an orphan. I live at the orphanage. I just took a walk so I could see what families do on Thanksgiving."

"Would you like to come to the monastery where I live and have a big Thanksgiving dinner with me? I don't have anybody either."

"Can I really?"

"Yes."

So, I drove him to the monastery and put together the meal the cook had prepared for those of us who would be there over Thanksgiving. I called the nun in charge of the orphanage and told her we were having Thanksgiving dinner together and I would bring him back as soon as dinner was over. She was happy I called and relieved that I had found him, as the sisters were worried.

But what about the little children who were unwanted from infancy, children just dumped into orphanages or on the doorsteps of foundling homes? Every now and then we would find babies left in the back pew of the church, abandoned by their mothers. It was heartbreaking.

One baby whose life I was able to follow was, as an infant, thrown into a garbage pail. Fortunately, someone found the poor baby and notified the sisters at an orphanage, who took the baby and cared for the child for a few years until they could find a worthy couple to adopt the child. My immediate thoughts were about what happens in the mind and in the soul of a child like that. Babies may not be fully aware of what is happening, but they can have feelings of being cared for, being secure, being loved—and of being frightened when left alone or abandoned. And they can experience fear and anxiety when that care, that security, and that love stops, and there is no one near to hug them and hold them. In their infant awareness they sense that someone who had been caring for them and loving them is gone. They can feel the devastating fright of being alone, even though they do not understand the meaning of the words *alone* or *abandoned.* They just know what it is.

Loving caregivers may step in and care for those infants, but the infants, as young as they are, can sense the difference, though they cannot define it. They sense more than we realize. One of my brothers had been seeing a psychoanalyst, who had him recall his memories as far back as he could. One day, to the psychoanalyst's surprise, my brother told him he remembered being born and that he was struggling to avoid being born. The doctor found it hard to believe. My brother told the story to our mother, who told him that his memory was correct, and that even her doctor was shocked that the baby had put up such a fight not to be born. My brother could remember the fear he had of being born and his struggle to prevent emerging into this world. Perhaps this was much like people's fear of dying and entering into the unknown.

There is a lot we do not know about childhood traumas and the effects these experiences have on children's personalities and their future responses to life's situations. A biography of Adolf Hitler describes the cruel beating his father unleashed on him practically every night, sometimes beating him into unconsciousness. Isn't that the way one trains attack dogs? His father, although partly Jewish, hated Jews and instilled in his son the same ha tred. Growing up deprived of love and any kind of tenderness, how could he have found the strength and depth of spirit to think and feel differently than the way he had been trained from childhood? How does a young boy develop a human heart after being trained to be a monster? If a child experiences love, the child can more easily learn to love. If a child experiences only hatred, what chance does that child have not to hate others?

Several men I know were severely beaten by their fathers. One man, as a little boy by the name of Joe, hardly nine years old at the time, went out for a walk one Sunday morning. When he returned, his father asked him where he had been. He told him that as he was walking up the street, he heard nice music and singing coming from the church. "So I went in and attended the services. It was nice. I felt peaceful." "Which church?" his father asked impatiently. "The Catholic church," the boy replied. The father then beat him unmercifully and forbade him ever to go near that church again.

The next Sunday the same thing happened, and for many Sundays after that. Every Sunday morning, when the boy came home from church, the father beat him brutally. When the boy grew older, he became a Catholic, joined the parish, and was very loyal to the church. Later, he became involved in labor issues, and represented International Harvester in labor negotiations with Jimmy Hoffa and the Teamsters Union, and was a tough negotiator.

I met this man many years later in Florida when I was on a speaking tour. He came into a bookstore where I was autographing books and immediately confronted me. He told me his name was Joe.

"You're a Catholic priest," he said. "How come every time you come down here, you speak only in Protestant churches?"

"Because they are the only ones who invite me. The Catholic churches don't want me."

"If our parish did invite you, would you come?"

"Of course. I'd love to."

Not long after, I got a phone call from Joe, telling me that he was authorized by his pastor to invite me to speak at their brand-new Catholic church. He asked if I would come.

"Of course. I told you I would."

We set the date for the series of five talks on a Saturday, starting at ten o'clock and ending at three o'clock. I flew from Albany, New York, to Naples, Florida. When I arrived, Joe met me at the airport. His wife, Mary, was with him—a most gracious lady. After a few pleasantries I asked Joe how he had managed to persuade the pastor to extend the invitation.

"That was easy. We had to get rid of the old wooden church after the new one was finished. I was put in charge of moving the building. The contractors fitted the building onto the huge flatbed. When they drove the truck off the land and into the middle of a busy intersection, I told the driver to stop. Pandemonium reigned. Soon the pastor came out and was beside himself with embarrassment and anger.

"What's the problem?" he asked.

"No problem," I replied. "We have to settle something first."

"What's that?" he asked me.

"What's it worth to you for me to get this thing moving again?"

"You wouldn't dare."

"Try me."

"All right. You're just miserable enough to do it. What do you want?"

"Permission to invite Father Joe Girzone down to speak in our parish."

"Damn you, Joe. You've pushed too far this time."

The horns kept honking, and the drivers kept screaming. A riot could easily have erupted. Joe clearly didn't care, so the pastor finally chickened out and said, "All right, you win. Go ahead and invite him, but you haven't heard the last of this."

"So, that's how I got you your invitation. Also, by the way, there is a man who will be sitting in the front row in the church for your talks. He is the one who was most vehemently opposed to you coming here, and he's a good friend of the pastor. Keep an eye on him."

"Boy, you're tough, Joe. It's hard to believe you would do a thing like that."

"Well, the pastor was a tough nut to crack, and he wouldn't give in, so I had to play hard ball and use one of my old last-ditch negotiating tactics. I was trained as a child to handle tough situations."

"Now I can see how you handled Jimmy Hoffa in your labor talks."

After spending time with Joe and Mary, he brought me down to the church for the talks.

"What about the pastor? Shouldn't we see him first out of courtesy?" I asked.

"Are you kidding? It'll be better if you meet him after the talks, when his friends will have told him good things about you and softened him up. He'll be in a much better frame of mind then."

"Joe, you're a genius."

"It's just a matter of knowing how to handle people."

My talks started on schedule, and I kept my eye on the man in the front row. Joe had described him very accurately, so I had no trouble recognizing him. All during the talk, "A New Sense of Jesus," he seemed in deep thought. And all during the remaining talks, until three o'clock in the afternoon, he had the same intense focus. At the end of the last talk he came up to me and told me very honestly that he had been vehemently opposed to my coming there, but after listening to what I had to say, his whole outlook on life and his religion had changed. With tears in his eyes he thanked me and said, "What a beautiful way to look at God and our Catholic faith." He apologized for judging me so harshly when he didn't even know me. I hugged him and laughed. I had a new friend.

After all the talks Joe brought me over to meet the pastor. It turned out just as Joe had predicted. The pastor's friends had brought him glowing reports of the talks, and thanked him for inviting me, which made the pastor feel proud. The pastor and I became good friends, and nothing was ever mentioned about how the invitation came about. I soon received invitations from other Catholic parishes in the area, and many told me that the talks were quite different from the rumors they had heard about me.

Joe's difficult childhood conditioned him to be tough, but it served to his benefit and to the benefit of many others all during his life. So, difficult and painful experiences can be the springboard to a strong character and healthy development of the personality. It was the Good Shepherd working in his soul from the first time he heard the music in that neighborhood church. God was inviting himself into that little boy's heart.

That Sunday morning when Joe, as a little boy, walked into that church and found peace made all the difference in his life. The peace he found in the feeling of being close to Jesus changed his life, and many years later he was thrilled to have the priest who wrote *Joshua* talk to his parish about Jesus.

One young man, who had had a horrendous childhood, hated his mother because of her promiscuous lifestyle and the cruel way she had treated him. He grew up with such a psychotic hatred of women that he ended up as a serial killer, brutally mutilating the bodies of his women victims. Can his behavior be traced to his childhood experiences? No one knows. It is easy to pass quick, offhanded judgments with the old comment, "Well, he had free will." But that's a cop out. For centuries moral theologians have recognized that there are many factors affecting free will; these factors can lessen guilt in varying degrees, even to the point of practically no guilt. Could it not also be true that there are some experiences that have so damaged a person mentally, emotionally, and psychologically that that person's will is incapable of resistance to violent impulses? Just as there is a limit to physical endurance, so there is also a limit to the will's endurance. That man's life in prison later on was touched by God's grace. The change was dramatic, and one might say, miraculous, all because of the quiet love of the Good Shepherd.

We do not ordinarily think of children as having pain, other than pain from illness or from bruised muscles or broken bones. But children suffer very much, most often from fears and anxiety. Children undergo a living hell when they hear their parents quarreling bitterly. The first thing that comes to children's mind these days is, "Are they going to get a divorce?" This makes it almost impossible for children to sleep. They often become prone to nightmares and subject to fears and guilt, thinking it may be their fault that their parents do not get along. "Maybe if I were better, they wouldn't fight so much." This is horrible for a child to go through. It robs them of the carefree joy that should be their heritage as children. Not only does it strip them of joy, it also does untold damage, emotionally and psychologically, that no one can really understand because children usually do not have the chance to explain what they feel or the ability to express their feelings even if someone is willing to listen.

Church is of little or no comfort to children, because clergy hardly ever talk about what is really relevant to children, about their pain, their problems, their fears, and their anxieties. They are fed bible stories or pious lessons while all the time they are going through hell in their souls. Adults like sermons that feed them, nourish them. Children would love to have someone talk to them about their childhood fears and hurts and pain. They would listen all day long if a priest or other clergyperson spoke to them about their childhood troubles. Their anxiety is just as real as the sufferings of adults, but children are more vulnerable than adults and do not know how to handle their emotional and psychological pain. All they know is that they feel terribly sick inside, and they don't know why. Their parents do not know either, as the children have no way of ventilating the terrible feelings that are making them so unhappy. Often the parents are so preoccupied with their own problems that they have little or no time or patience to unravel their children's problems. The children are then thrown totally upon themselves. That is dangerous, because no one can begin to fathom how, with their lack of experience, they are handling their pain and childhood disillusion. They might resort to behavior that they subconsciously know will upset their parents, often to get their attention, to make their parents realize the damage they are doing to them by the way they are acting. If they know their parents are religious, they might then turn against religion to frighten their parents into waking up to all the harm they are causing, or because they are really disillusioned with God for allowing such terrible things to happen, and for permitting their secure world to fall apart.

Sometimes, though not very often, a child may find God or a warm feeling about Jesus or his Blessed Mother. Occasionally a child may react like Saint Thérèse, who, after the death of her mother, used to isolate herself in her canopied bed to think about God and pray. In this way she found comfort and a feeling of intimacy with God that gave her peace. It also made her feel closer to her mother. This tender relationship with God blossomed as she grew older and, after becoming a Carmelite nun, she became one of the most highly venerated saints of our time, canonized shortly after her death at an early age.

While it may seem rare that a child should have such a relationship with God that could affect his or her whole life in a beautiful and healthy way, it does show what potential lies beneath the surface of a child's life if parents are sensitive to what their children are experiencing and are willing to help them understand themselves. It does take careful attention to a child's moods and reactions along with the ability to make the child feel comfortable enough to share his or her feelings. But the rewards of helping the child learn to handle pain and childhood frustrations are great.

We instinctively associate childhood with a time of joy, happiness, and a beautiful life free of care. It is difficult for us to realize that life for children is not that simple or carefree, even in a country where there are so many reasons for children to be happy and free of worry. It is surprising how many children do not like themselves. The reasons they feel that way are countless. In comparison with others they often feel either ugly, stupid, clumsy, or unlikable; they see themselves as unloved, and worse, unlovable. They may not express this to anyone, but they think it, and it occupies a good part of their conscious hours. It also shows up in their dreams, often in symbolic images.

The variety of problems that trouble youngsters is unending, but I would like to share with you a story of another young boy who is like so many of his type. He was not academically gifted, but he had rare abilities. One day he poured his heart out to me. He told me that he felt he was stupid, that he had a hard time in school, and that he knew he was a disappointment to his parents, who were professional people and well respected in the community. When I asked him if he studied hard, he said that he tried, but it was difficult for him because he could not understand what the teacher was talking about. I could understand the boy because I couldn't understand what my teachers were talking about in English class, though I was good in other subjects. Then I asked him if there was anything he liked to do, and he told me he liked to draw and paint pictures, but that his parents told him he could never make a living at that and he should get an education first so he could get a good job. "Is there anything else you like to do?" I asked him. "Yes, I like to fix toys and little machines."

"How do you do that?"

"I take them apart to see how they are made, and then I put them back together again. Sometimes, when I was first learning, I didn't do a good job at putting them back together, but I learned. Now I'm good at it."

"So, you see you are not stupid. You have a talent for something that most people can't even understand. Some people can read books and like to learn what they find in books and in schoolwork, but others have different gifts. When you get older, you will probably be able to get a good job working on cars, or machinery, or engines. You may even be able to design your own engines."

When I said that he beamed, and said, "I would love to do that kind of work."

"Well, stop saying or even thinking that you are stupid. You are not stupid. You are blessed with a great talent. There are people who may not have been good at schoolwork but were talented at art, business, or other fields. The world looks upon some of them as geniuses. So, learn to like yourself. You have great potential, and even if you don't think you are good in school, do the best you can, and don't be too easy on yourself in your schoolwork.

What you learn will always be a big help to you later on. Don't let school time be a waste of time. It is precious, and you will learn even if you don't get the highest marks in the class. You are still learning important things you will use later on. And always remember, God gave you all the talents you need to do a very special work for him. You may not know now what that work is, but God will always be your partner, helping you all along the way, like today, when you found someone to share your problem with."

Just that simple chat made all the difference in the world for that young boy. Talking to his parents was all that was needed to help them understand and not do unnecessary damage to his self-image by putting pressure on him to be what they wanted him to be. Parents must respect what God has given to their children and not demand of them beyond what God has given. It is so important that children have a healthy feeling about themselves, and this can be undermined by parents' unreasonable demands. It is too bad that school officials and educators don't recognize the latent talent in the vast number of students who are not academically blessed but have rich talents in areas that are so necessary for the enrichment of our society. Students should be tested for their talents when they are young and provided with the chance to develop what God has given them. There would be many more happy young people and a lot less crime.

One of the worst difficulties endured by many children is abuse by parents. This is more common than people imagine. It is not limited just to fathers. Mothers can also be responsible for abuse of a child. The majority of childhood abuse is committed within families, not by outsiders, even though the news media and the public seem to focus mostly on child abuse by clergy. That is, surprisingly, where the violations are probably among the lowest. One police official told me that over the years he was shocked at the high incidence of child abuse on the part of police officers. And sexual abuse is not limited to clergy and police officers. This is a widespread problem among groups at all levels of society. But, perhaps, the highest percentage of sexual-abuse cases involves fathers abusing their own children or men abusing nephews and nieces. This is so sad, and when you realize how prevalent it is, it is easy to understand why there are so many dysfunctional adults as a result. The effects on the child are devastating and long lasting.

I was once asked if I would help nine young ladies in their twenties and early thirties to write a book. When I asked them what kind of a book, I was told that they were sisters, and all nine had been sexually abused by their father when they were children. They felt the only way they could be healed of their horrifying memories and what the abuse had done to them was to process their experiences by writing about them. At the time I felt I was inadequate to be of any honest professional assistance. Fortunately, their aunt was a very spiritual nun who was a great help in the healing process.

As time passed I kept learning more and more about the damage done to childhood victims of such abuse, and it was painful to deal with it. Victims of such abuse have a very difficult time developing trust. If a boy has been abused by his mother or another woman, he has difficulty relating to female friends. If a girl has been abused, she has difficulties relating to male friends. There are just too many unresolved emotional and psychological problems that have to be processed. Often they turn out to be insurmountable, and marriages very frequently break up because of the inability to process the many problems involved.

Occasionally, a person, usually a woman, has been able to work through her traumatic experience, although she may hate her father and find it impossible to understand why he did what he did. She may find it almost impossible to forgive him, because of the scars she knows she will carry for the rest of her life. However, I have met with women who for the most part successfully dealt with what they experienced and later decided to spend the rest of their lives dedicated to helping young girls who had been abused by parents. They were able to help these young women resolve their issues and reach a point where they could successfully relate to men in a healthy manner and develop relaxed and enjoyable relationships with men and eventually with a husband.

In such difficult and traumatic experiences, the person's relationship with God has to be healed, because there is so much guilt felt by the victim, especially since we look upon God as father. Their image of father has been so badly damaged that it is very difficult for a person, especially a woman, who has been abused to feel comfortable with God as father. They often cringe at the thought of it. A compassionate priest or other clergyperson can, with time and patience, and great understanding, convince the person that she, or he, is not evil because of what was done to them, but that God understands their terrible suffering and feels only sympathy and compassion for what they have gone through. God does not want them to feel guilt over what they have suffered. In time, once such individuals feel comfortable with God and can begin to pray again, God can take over and, knowing that they are now at peace with God, they can begin to forgive themselves and be at peace with themselves. It is a long and painful process, but it can be successful, even though the feelings of shame may last for a long time. The important thing to remember is that healing is possible, if a person is willing to work at it and not decide to go through life as a permanent victim.

With the wide experience I have had with issues like this, and other issues that cause lasting damage, I was able to understand what a vast number of seriously damaged people there are; even as adults they are still very fragile. As a result I realized that when these fragile people finally get the courage to approach a priest hoping to reconcile with the church, and receive communion, it is important that we are open to accepting them where they are at and not insist on further unnecessary demands before allowing Jesus to embrace them in communion. Communion should be not only a reward for the holy but also medicine for the sick, who desperately are reaching out to Jesus. If such a fragile person met Jesus on the street, can anyone imagine him giving the person a hard time before allowing him to hug him? Can any of us imagine Jesus saying, "Keep away from me until you are healed of your sickness?"

A young man I'll call Scott did not remember his parents. His memories of childhood consisted of being sent to different homes and not feeling liked or loved. He often just wandered the streets. He always felt he was a nuisance to his caregivers, until one day he found an old lady who liked him. She took him in and was like a mother to him. She was the first real mother he ever had, but being so old she did not live long. When she died, Scott felt a terrible rage that she had been taken from him. She was the only person who ever had loved him, and now she was no more. She was gone. Now he had nobody and felt totally alone in the world. That had to be painful and frightening. His fright turned to anger, then rage. Later on he married and found himself responsible for a wife and two children, whom he admits he did not treat well. He was abusive. Love and tenderness were traits he never had learned, so he acted the way he had always been

treated during so much of his early life. It was all
he knew.

Eventually, Scott ended up in prison for seriously
violent crimes, and to this day he still has feelings
of rage. When he contacted me, it was after another
inmate had befriended him and introduced him to
Joshua and *Never Alone.* These books opened for
him a door to a whole world of new possibilities.
He learned that there is one person who loves him,
cares for him, and understands him, and even his
rage, and that's Jesus. So, he has begun to develop
a simple, down-to-earth friendship with Jesus and
now shares everything in his life with him. This relationship is not a "corny" fantasy. It is a real manly
friendship that inspires this young man to want to
better his life, even when he feels so much rage.

At first he was afraid that he would never be
able to overcome his rage. He was even afraid to
be released from prison because he did not know
whether he had the discipline to live peacefully. Now
he knows that, when he shares his rage with Jesus,
he feels a peace he has never known and feels confi-
dent he can, with God's help, overcome and control
his propensity for violence. He is finally beginning
to believe he can go out into the community again
and live a productive life.

With a renewed enthusiasm for bettering his life,
he is studying scripture with the help of a good
scriptural commentary and reading other good
books. Gradually, his life is changing. He feels
himself becoming stronger, which shows that even
those severely damaged from childhood can find

hope and strength when introduced to someone who cares and is willing to be there for support. Rehabilitation is not something to be sneered at, as it is by some people. Rehabilitation is much more pleasing to God than the hatred and vindictiveness that have become so much a part of our national culture and supposedly enlightened society, in which the need to destroy sinners is nothing more than a thinly disguised hatred of God's damaged children. And often people with this mentality pride themselves on being good Christians and concerned citizens.

Another man I know, who is a dear friend, told me the story of his life. He lived in the wooded mountains of North Carolina with his four brothers. Jack was the second oldest. The oldest was fifteen. The youngest was about five. The two others were between ten and eight. Their mother had died, and their father was a perpetual alcoholic who rarely came home from the bar where he spent his time after work.

I asked Jack how they could possibly take care of themselves. He said, "We just had to, so we learned. We couldn't go to a store and get food, so we had to figure how we were going to eat. We learned how to make bows and arrows and hunt rabbits and squirrels. We found that we could get quail eggs from their nests hidden in the grass. When it rained at night, we listened to the birds chirping, and the next morning we looked around where we had heard the chirping and we found the eggs, so we had eggs for breakfast.

"Were you lonely?"

"Well, we missed mother. Father was never there anyway. But we had so much fun playing and looking for food, we didn't have time to feel sorry for ourselves."

"What did you do for fun?"

"We climbed trees and swung from branch to branch like monkeys, seeing how far we could swing before we fell. Whoever went the farthest won."

"Didn't you get hurt when you fell?"

"Yeah, it hurt, but we didn't break anything. It was no different than kids playing football. You get hurt, but that's part of the game."

"Did you go to school?"

"Never missed a day! I knew that that was going to be my ticket out of there."

"What was school like?"

"Same as it was for any kid. Only, one problem every day was lunchtime. The teacher would say, "All the poor kids, see me at lunchtime so you can get your lunch. But I was too proud to admit I was poor, so I never had lunch. I'd go and pick berries or find other things in the woods I could eat, then come back for afternoon classes."

"What was it like in your house in the winter?"

"Cold."

"How did you survive?"

"It wasn't much of a house, just a shack. You could see outside through the spaces between the boards. It was freezing in the winter. My father started the place when our mother was alive but never finished it. We had a potbelly stove and filled it with wood we collected during the fall. We had one big blanket, and a dog. We put the dog in the middle, and we all slept around the dog. The dog was always warm, and the blanket covered most of our bodies, but part of us was always exposed to the cold. When the fire went out, we just waited for the sun to come up."

"What did you do for clothes?"

"We went down to our grandfather's house and asked him if he needed any work done. He would never just give us clothes. He always said it was our father's job to take care of us, not his job, but if we worked for him, he would give us some clothes. That's how we got our clothes."

"How did you finally get out of there?"

"I graduated from high school."

"What did you do then?"

"I enlisted in the army."

"What did you do in the army?"

"They assigned me to the intelligence corps."

"The intelligence corps?"

"Yes, the intelligence corps. They saw that I noticed every little thing that happened and never forgot it, so they tested me and said I would be good at intelligence. You've got to remember we grew up like little animals, watching everything just for survival, and most people don't grow up with that kind of awareness of every little detail of everything that happens around them. Our officers noticed that and said I would be perfect for intelligence work."

"And when you left the army?"

"I became a civil planner, then married, and got religion. I started going to church with my wife,

Nancy. Church was nice. It made me feel peaceful, and God felt very close. I just liked being there. The others were always complaining about something or other, about this priest who can't speak, or that one who can't sing, or that mass is boring. I don't know what's bothering them. I just enjoy being there. I couldn't care less what's going on around me. I'm there. God's there, and when God comes in communion, what more could anyone want? I think people *make* themselves discontented. Why can't they just enjoy the beautiful miracle of God being with us?"

That was the life of my friend Jack. He was born with nothing, had nothing most of his young life, yet still found life a happy adventure. One last thing I asked him was about his father. "Did you like your father, Jack?"

"For a long time I didn't. But one day he came out on his bicycle and told me to get on the handlebar, and he would take me for a ride. We rode along the bumpy path through the woods, and along the way, my father kept singing, like he had not a care in the world. Then all of a sudden he lost control, and we tipped over and fell into a ditch. He fell sound asleep, and I just lay there next to him. It was the only time I was physically close to my father. And I knew he loved me because he came all the way from town to take me for a bicycle ride, and I felt sorry for the poor man, and I realized for the first time that when mother died, his life fell apart. He just couldn't cope with life after that. From that day I never resented him, because I finally knew he loved me but was too weak to be of any use to us. From then on, I just felt sorry that his life was so sad."

What a beautiful soul is reflected in this true life story! No bitterness, no regrets over a life deprived of all the good things, just simple joy and happiness in the enjoyment of life's difficult adventure, and the remarkable peace in being close to God, when he finally found him. Jack's life shows vividly the care and love of the Good Shepherd, who was gently guiding him through life until he finally found peace and a home in God's love.

3

Suffering from Feeling Different from Everybody Else

One day at a wedding party I met a guest rolling around in his wheelchair. He was a man in his early fifties, a pleasant fellow, and very sociable. We spent a good bit of time chatting, and he pretty much told me the story of his life.

Let's call him Bill. Bill was born deformed, especially his legs, which he was never able to use. He was totally dependent on others for his whole childhood. He told me he was one of those kids whom some say should be aborted, because they will be of no use to anybody and a lifelong burden to others. "But, I proved them all wrong," he said. "I was determined to make something of myself. Now, I am one of the top engineers in the state. I am proud that people respect me for my ability as an engineer. My mother and father were proud of me and enthused about what I was able to accomplish before they died. It has not been easy, but I was determined not to give up until I accomplished what I set out to do, and that was to get a good education and one day become an engineer—not just any kind of an engineer, but a damned good one. I thank God for helping me all along the way. My parents are dead now, and I am not married, so it can be lonely at times, but, as a priest, you know that being alone can be good if you have a lot of interests. So, I have a happy life, and I enjoy the comradeship of my friends. What more could a person want in life, if he has peace and happiness?"

By the time he finished, I was deeply impressed with what he shared, and told him that he had to have been an inspiration to many he met along the way during his life, and that I, too, was inspired by what he had told me.

Even though what he said may have sounded like boasting, it was a justifiable pride and a humble expression of his own wonder that he really did accomplish his seemingly impossible dreams.

Since that day I have thought about what his childhood must have been like. Unable to walk would be devastating for any child. To be totally dependent on others would undermine even a strong child's feeling of self-worth. Not being able to walk over to a refrigerator and get something you want, not being able to turn on a radio or a television unless you have a remote, not being able to pick up something you dropped, falling and not being able to get up. Not being able to help yourself in so many little ways all day long could test a child's desire to live, much less look forward to enjoying a long life, with the specter of frightening loneliness after parents die.

Imagine the embarrassment of not being able to get out of bed in the morning or during the night without having to call somebody for help. Unless a severely handicapped child has very loving parents, the child could be destroyed, even if it is only from neglect or not anticipating the child's needs, so he or she doesn't have to call and ask for every little thing.

But even though Bill experienced all the horrors of being unable to move from place to place and needed twenty-four hour assistance, he never became bitter or resentful. He was determined to make his disability the motivation for what were to be for him, and indeed for anyone, great accomplishments. And he succeeded.

With a severe problem like this, some people become bitter, resenting life's difficulties as cruel and unjust on the part of a God who is supposed to love. Others accept the challenge and not only overcome their handicaps but develop a heroic sanctity in the process of attaining their dreams. Some of the greatest artists and architects were severely handicapped. Demosthenes, the great Greek philosopher and orator, had a stuttering problem as a youth, which, by sheer persistence, he was able to conquer and become one of the greatest of the ancient orators. Winston Churchill was handicapped by bipolar disorder, a victim of wide mood swings and weird behavior, who, in spite of his problem, led his country to victory against seemingly insurmountable obstacles and air attacks by a military power determined to destroy his country.

Some of the greatest geniuses were schizophrenic, like John Nash, who won the Nobel Prize for economics, and who struggled for a lifetime with the horrible disease. Another tragic illness is autism. A dear friend of mine who is autistic is a mathematical genius. He can solve the most complex mathematical problems without a piece of paper or calculator of any kind. The inability of an uncreative society to create ways to develop and put to good use all this genius is the real cause of so much heartache and frustration for these talented people. This beautiful young man has the most tender love of God; to hear him talk about God would touch the heart of the worst skeptic.

What makes the difference in the lives of the children who were victims of others' meanness is how they respond to this painful treatment. Some nurse their hurts all the rest of their lives, and in their old age still live in bitterness and hatred of others, totally forgetful of the mean things they themselves have done to others. They live lives of unforgiveness, convincing themselves of their own innocence, which they must protect against the meanness of their family or others. Often their wounds are imaginary, stemming more from an overly sensitive personality than from hurts intentionally inflicted by parents or siblings, who frequently care deeply for them though they cannot understand their behavior. I have seen this often as a priest. It is a common problem in many families.

Now I will share with you still another true story that has always been an inspiration for me. I read this short biography many years ago when I was studying history, and I was so impressed by it that, even though some of the details may be vague, I can still remember the important details very vividly.

During a time when there were still kings and queens and castles, and knights in shining armor and beautiful ladies in waiting, there was also a baby boy born to a poor family who worked near the royal estate. Sigismund was born with arms and legs that were only partially developed and barely useful. He was the type of baby for whom some "enlightened" people today would consider it the ultimate expression of compassion to terminate his life.

But Sigismund's parents were determined that if God entrusted this child to them, there must be a reason for it, and a purpose to the child's life. So, they cared for that baby with extraordinary love and solicitude. As he grew older they noticed that Sigismund was very bright and had a prodigious memory. He loved to listen to stories and was eager to learn. His great comfort was listening to music he heard coming from the castle grounds, especially when there were parties. As the boy grew older, his parents realized that the child's only enjoyment in life would be in the use of his mind, so they arranged for him to learn to read. They found kind persons who could read, and who were only too happy to take turns reading to him and helping him to understand what was read. In every age there are caring people who are kind enough to reach out to others, and so it was in the life of Sigismund. There were people in the neighborhood of the castle who had received an education from the monks, and they enjoyed being with Sigismund because he was so intelligent and had such a craving to learn. Not only did these people teach him to read, but they also taught him mathematics and history. As he grew in age, monks from the Benedictine monastery took turns teaching him philosophy, science, Latin and Greek, and most important, a deeper understanding of the faith his parents had taught him in their simple way when he was a child. His very difficult life forced him to draw within himself and try to understand the meaning of life, particularly his own life. One of the monks helped Sigismund to understand that his life was precious and was intimately tied up in the mystery of God's purpose for him, and that in time he would see the beautiful way that God was using him, as he uses everyone to better the lives of others, even persons we do not know. In the process of his meditations and with the help of the monks he developed a profound wisdom, which is often the fruit of long suffering that forces a person inward in a desperate attempt to understand the meaning of life on earth and the relevance of God.

As a young man Sigismund was known for miles around as the freak with the brilliant mind. In time the young man's reputation for learning spread far beyond the borders of his country, and learned people came just to talk to him and ask his opinion on many difficult matters. The king himself, who had been hearing about this young prodigy, could not believe that he lived right in the shadow of the castle. One day he sent two courtiers to the humble home where this man lived with his aging parents, who were finding it more and more difficult to care for their crippled son, and were beside themselves with worry about what would happen to him when they died. Day and night they begged God to care for the child he had entrusted to them, reminding God that Sigismund was his child and they, as his parents, were only caring for this special boy who really belonged to God.

Their prayers were not ignored. When the courtiers knocked at the door of the little hovel where the boy and his parents lived, the old couple were shocked and frightened to see these two important looking men, who promptly told them that they were courtiers sent by the king to talk with them. The old man invited them in, placed near the table two simple chairs he had made, and gestured for them to be seated. The courtiers were most gracious and said they would not take much time, as they could see that the couple had much work to do.

They immediately explained the purpose of their visit. "His majesty, King Siegfried, has heard wonderful things about your brilliant son and would very much like to meet with him. Would it be possible for us to meet with your son, so we can bring information back to his majesty?"

"Yes, of course," the old man replied. He and his wife invited the two visitors into a room where the young man was propped up in a special chair constructed in such a way that it could hold his body erect.

When they entered, they were shocked at seeing the frightfully crippled condition of the young man. "Do you have another son?" one of the courtiers asked.

"No, he is the only one the good Lord has blessed us with. God sure did give us a treasure."

After talking with the young man for a few minutes, the visitors were astonished at the brilliance of this pitiable being sitting there so helpless. What impressed them even more was the humility that cloaked this brilliant mind. After a few minutes the visitors took their leave and returned to the king and shared with him what they had experienced as well as their concern for the boy who was totally helpless. His aging parents would probably not be able to care for him much longer.

The king was impressed with what he had been told. Soon he sent his two closest advisers to visit the parents and inform them that the king would very much like to have their son live in the castle and be one of the king's advisers. The parents would also be expected to live in the castle and have their own private quarters, and would be well cared for, until such time as God saw fit to take them home.

The couple was filled with deep and confusing emotions and did not know what to say or how to respond. The king had surmised that that would be the reaction, so the messengers were instructed to insist that these were the king's wishes and that they should ready themselves for the move within two days. Servants would transport them and their belongings to the castle. They could bring with them whatever possessions they wished.

Once settled in the castle, and thanking God for his great kindness, they received a message from the king that he wanted to meet Sigismund.

Servants would come to escort him to the king's chambers. The king knew that the young man was crippled but was surprised to see just how helpless his condition was and was more shocked at his happy and peaceful personality and his sense of humor. After just a few minutes of conversation, and questions about difficult matters, the king was astonished that this stump of a human person could be blessed with such intelligence. The more complex the questions the king asked, the more amazed he was at the young man's brilliance. He could not but wonder where all this man's wisdom came from. Is it something he learned on his own, or did his wisdom come directly from God?

As the days passed the king's counselors briefed Sigismund each day on all the business of the kingdom and the complex details of the king's relationships with his own nobles as well as neighboring monarchs. The young man learned fast and never forgot a detail of what he had been taught.

It was not long before the king summoned his new counselor and presented him with an issue that had haunted him for years, causing many sleepless nights. It involved a neighboring king, Konrad, who was forever threatening invasion of Siegfried's lands and made no secret of his hatred for him. Siegfried responded in kind. Both knew that it was just a matter of time before violence would erupt and both their countries would be reduced to ashes.

Siegfried explained the complicated problem to the young man and asked what he thought could be done to resolve this impossible situation. Sigismund thought for a few moments, looked up into the king's eyes, and said, "Your majesty, if you really want to resolve this seemingly impossible situation, pray hard and with God's help, all you need to do is just one thing."

"What is that, Sigismund?"

"No longer look upon King Konrad as your enemy but as a person who needs something very badly and is ashamed to ask."

"What is it that he wants or needs."

"That is what you will have to find out?"

"And how will I ever find that out?"

"By a simple act of humility. Send a messenger to the king and humbly ask his help. He may act haughty to cover his pride, but still he will be most curious to know what it is you need. You will then have a chance to suggest a peaceful meeting between the two of you. I would suggest you invite him to dinner at your summer home in the mountains, with each of you accompanied by only a few attendants."

"But I need nothing from that man."

"I beg your forgiveness, your majesty, but you do. Your dear wife, the queen, is very sick, and you have no doctor in your kingdom as learned as that man's doctor. Even if it matters little to him whether your queen lives or dies, he will not refuse to help, because he will be in a position to reveal to you what he also needs, which had been at the heart of your conflict with him all these years."

The messengers were sent, and the scenario unfolded just as Sigismund had predicted. The two kings met, and after a dinner they both enjoyed, they shared their tales of woe. Siegfried explained the seriousness of his wife's illness and expressed how grateful he would be if Konrad could help him by loaning him his doctor. When the king agreed, Siegfried humbly asked if there was any way he could express his gratitude.

"Yes, as a matter of fact, I do have a great need that I have never been able to discuss with you, even though I knew you could help."

"What is that?"

"Part of my country that is adjacent to your border suffers severe drought on a regular basis, and I have no way of providing water for all those people who live there. I was always so envious of you having that huge lake fed by the glacier on top of the mountain, but I could never get myself to admit I may need, so I just hated you. Since you had the humility to ask for my help, I now have the humility to ask you if you could help me and my people. I would be so grateful."

"I would be more than happy to help in something so important to your people. I will instruct my men to start working on that immediately."

The two men became best friends from that very day. In time the king's wife was healed of her illness, and the lands across the border were rich with abundant harvests every year thereafter.

Sigismund lived a long life, and his reputation as the king's counselor spread throughout Europe. Kings, bishops, cardinals, and scholars came from great distances to spend just a few precious moments with the rare handicapped man with a wisdom that could only come from God. His life was the wonder and inspiration not only to the king, but to people far and wide. God often bestows his greatest gifts on those some consider of little value. Perhaps we will meet them one day.

There are other childhood sufferings that come not from missing limbs or physical disabilities but from differences that may have their source in a complicated genetic structure. As a priest all kinds of people come to share their heart's deepest concerns. A long time ago a young man shared with me that he was gay and asked me if I thought there was something wrong with him.

I asked him when he first realized he was gay, and he told me that he always felt different, even as a young boy. He told me that when he was a child he used to like to play with dolls, play house with his sisters, and was not attracted to sports. "I would have thought nothing of this if my father didn't call me a sissy and start being mean to me. He kept saying, 'I'll make a man out of you yet.' And he began punishing me for playing with dolls and doing other things my sisters liked to do. My brothers also began making fun of me and calling me names, which I didn't understand."

"How old were you then?" I asked him.

"I think I must have been about four, not quite five, but as I got older, I still had more fun doing the things that my sisters enjoyed doing, and we got along well. I seemed to think and feel the way they did about a lot of things, and at the same time I was less comfortable with my brothers. I liked nice clothes and liked to dress well; my brothers didn't care what they wore, and they were always getting dirty. I used to get upset if my clothes got dirty. I didn't like playing sports with my brothers. I tried, but I just didn't enjoy it. It wasn't fun for me. Besides, the boys were too rough. I could see why the girls didn't want to play with them either."

"Did you feel you are different in any other ways?"

"No, not at that age, but when I became a teenager, I noticed that I was more attracted to boys and didn't want to play with the girls anymore. I started to like boys, some more than others. I also noticed that when I liked a particular boy, I wanted to see him more often, and when I couldn't be with him, I was sad and terribly lonely. I didn't feel that way about girls, and I didn't have the same fun with girls that I had when I was younger. At the time I didn't think anything about it. I just felt certain boys were better friends than others, and it never struck me as being odd. But one boy I liked so much that I felt I couldn't live without him, and I became so sad when I saw he had a girlfriend, and I was so jealous of that girl. I wanted him to love me and not her. It was only then that I began to realize that something seemed not right, and I got panicky, and from then on I knew there was something different about me. The other boys were finding girlfriends, and I was looking for a boyfriend.

"Father, is there something wrong with me?"

"Charlie, there is nothing wrong with you. What you notice about yourself *is* you. What you are is God's gift to you, and God doesn't make mistakes. It is not easy to be different from so many others, but you are not alone. If you don't feel comfortable being the way you are, you could get years of therapy, but it may not change anything. Occasionally it may, if the problem is not too deeply genetic, and I am no one to judge. You have to decide what route you want to take.

"If you choose to live the way you are, be very careful whom you choose as friends. Be very careful and very wary. There are many who just use others for their own selfish reasons and may not be loyal or faithful friends. Also, if you are not careful, the lifestyle can be dangerous. And do not be too trusting of anyone who wants to be your friend."

We had a long conversation, back and forth, and I hope I conveyed to Charlie what I tried to share with other men and women I counseled in the future: how we are made is often the key to God's plan for our destiny in life.

"You have talents that others who are different from you lack. These traits go with the way you are and are part of the gifts God has given to you so you will be equipped to do the very special work God has planned for you. So, accept God as your partner and ask him to guide you through your life. You will find God a kind and nonjudgmental companion throughout your life; he will overlook your faults and weaknesses just as he overlooks the faults and weaknesses of all of us. You have a beautiful life ahead of you. Face it with assurance that you were given what you need to do a very special work for God, a work that is necessary to fill some important need in society. You are a special creation with a special job. Be proud, and don't torment yourself over how you are, but just be very careful for your own sake. We all have to be disciplined in controlling our feelings. You are going to have to be particularly disciplined. And always remember, God loves you as he made you. You have been blessed with a personality that has a rare sensitivity to people, and also a good mind, and with the talents that God has given to you, you are in a position to accomplish things you would never be able to do if you were different from what you are, so love the difference that God has given you and let God use you to accomplish his dreams for you."

I never saw Charlie after that. He told me before he left that he felt very much at peace with what I had said, and his mind was finally settled. He did tell me that he knew he was going to have to be very close to God, because he was still afraid of making bad decisions in his life.

I have grown to understand how different God is from us and how far beyond our thinking are his ways. Having known so many men and women, I have learned to appreciate that God needs the specific and unique kind of abilities and talents that are special to gay and lesbian people—though I could never determine whether God planned their lives this way or whether God just accepted what had happened in nature and made adjustments in order to give them the capability for very productive lives and the chance to make important contributions to better the lives of others, sometimes all across the world. I feel it is an insulting affront to God to cast off these blessed and gifted souls as if they are pariahs and unacceptable.

Guilt is a terrible burden for any of us to bear, and it is surely a sin to burden another with guilt. Guilt is not good. Guilt doesn't work. Only perfect love casts out guilt and fear.

Guilt carries with it emotional and psychological and even psychosomatic suffering that is almost universal and damaging in many ways. As I learned from professionals, most people seeking psychiatric help do so as a way of managing or getting rid of guilt. I have learned from hearing confessions all my priestly life what great relief individuals experience when they confess a problem or something they have done, or something they should have done and did not do. The sigh of relief that comes from them is almost humorous. And it is real. But the pain and suffering that come from guilt repressed over many years take a serious toll on people. We have all been taught how to live with integrity and honesty. When we violate those ideas, it immediately affects us, even as little children. As a child I was happy to go to confession and tell God I was sorry for doing things I should not have done. When I received absolution from the priest I knew that I was really at peace with God, because he gave the power to the apostles to forgive sin and said that when they forgave sin the sin was forgiven. I always walked away from confession as free as the wind. I can only imagine how miserable I would have been if I could not have unburdened my conscience of those sins, which were not really great but still troubled me because I was not living the way I should.

As a priest I learned from confession the anguish people go through. I also learned a lot outside confession when people told me that they had committed terrible sins and were too ashamed to go to confession, and felt that telling God wasn't enough, because they had tried it but they still did not find peace. What I would do then is suggest that they come to confession and not say anything. Instead, I would ask them questions; all they had to say was yes or no. From long experience I learned how many horrible and shameful things are done, so my asking questions always shocked the people by how much I knew, but it worked. They found it easy just to say, yes or no to whatever sins I listed and that they were too ashamed of putting into words themselves, but they answered properly when I asked the questions. At the end I encouraged them to relax and asked if they were sorry for what they had done. Of course they were, and they were so relieved that that part of their life was past history, that their repentance was sincere and powerful. Their relief from that terrible burden of guilt was immediate, and they would often break down in tears just from the freedom they felt after getting all that pent-up guilt out of their system.

I think the most powerful healing that Jesus performed while on earth was when he forgave people's sins and took away the horrible burden of guilt they suffered. I think that power to forgive sin has the same effect on penitents today as it did when Jesus was on earth. And his healing forgiveness passes from the heart of the Good Shepherd today through his human instruments in many powerful ways as in his time on earth long ago.

In all of these heartbreaking stories of people suffering from severe self-judgment and feeling different from everyone else, it is clear that deep faith made the difference in all their lives. Although many people discount the value of faith in God and have little or no understanding of the value of God in their lives, it is so transparent to persons with open minds and hearts who work closely with these struggling and hurting sheep, how much their faith and intimacy with God plays in their lives, and the strength and vision and courage that drives them to accomplish remarkable feats against unimaginable odds. Suffering may be inevitable, but God does make a difference!

4

Suffering in Adulthood

Sometimes I wonder. Suffering is everywhere. No one escapes it. Can anyone ever find happiness?

A year after ordination I was assigned to a parish in the Bronx. While on duty one Sunday, I went over to the church in the afternoon to lock up. Kneeling at the Blessed Mother's altar was a lady in her late thirties, dressed in black, with a delicately crocheted Spanish veil over her blond hair. She seemed troubled, so I walked up to her and asked her if she was all right. She looked at me and asked if she could please come and talk with me.

I locked the church, and we went over to the priory, which is what they call a rectory where monks live, and she poured out her heart for over an hour. She was married to a wonderful man, a Jewish man who was corporate counsel for RCA. She had been in and out of psychiatric hospitals and under the care of psychiatrists for years. All I could do was listen, as I had no in-depth training in psychiatry. The more she shared, the more inadequate I felt to help. I was just a young priest out of the seminary for only a year. I had never dealt with problems of the kind she was sharing with me. All I could do was feel her pain. And I could not imagine how a woman so beautiful could be so troubled.

After that session she asked if she could come and talk to me again, and over the next year or so she shared much of her life. I was introduced to pain and anguish at a really deep level. It was the first time I had experienced a person suffering such inner turmoil. After all the sessions we had during over a year and a half, she seemed finally to be at peace. One Sunday afternoon the phone rang. It was the lady's husband. He wanted to thank me for helping his wife to find peace. He knew I would never take money for all those sessions, so he said he would like to take me for a ride on his yacht, which he had moored out in Long Island Sound.

Helping that woman was the beginning of many such sessions with others for the next fifty-five years. Every week people came to the rectory to share with me the complex and frightening problems in their lives. What I had never learned from books I was now learning from real life, as people laid bare their souls, sharing with me a whole new world of pain and suffering that I had never imagined existed. This was invaluable from a spiritual perspective because it helped me to understand why Jesus referred to himself as the Good Shepherd, and what he meant by a good shepherd and by troubled, bruised, and hurting sheep. What I was learning gradually on a day-to-day basis, Jesus knows fully—the pain and anguish people suffer throughout the world. He not only knows people's pain, but as Isaiah said, he came to take upon himself the burden of our sins and our pain. I was beginning to understand that as well, because I found myself carrying the pain of those I tried to help. What Isaiah said concerns a mystery: that God can and does share our pain, and the heavy burden caused by the evil in the world. I was gradually learning that one cannot be a good shepherd until one has experienced the universal pain in people's souls, as Jesus could understand and share our pain.

People may ask: "How can God share our pain? That means God is with us in our pain and that means God suffers. How can God suffer, since suffering means enduring things you have no control over?"

To understand a little of how God suffers, I think we have to realize that God does not experience our suffering in the way we experience suffering. We may have no control over suffering, but that is different from the way God handles our suffering. When we say he takes upon himself our suffering, it does not mean that God endures the same human frustration and anxiety that comes from our human impotence to handle our problems. It means that God takes upon himself the responsibility to be with us, to care for us in our suffering, and to give us the grace to draw strength and spiritual growth and wisdom from our suffering, while molding in us the heroic image of Jesus. Mark expressed Jesus' concern for people's difficult lives on the occasion of the first multiplication of the loaves and fishes. He said Jesus "had compassion on them, because they were like sheep without a shepherd."

That was not an empty expression by a person who merely felt pity for someone's hopeless situation but did nothing. Jesus' compassion was a caring awareness of their hunger and hopelessness and how much they needed him and an intimacy with God. And immediately he set about doing something to show this care and fed their souls for the rest of the afternoon and then fed them with a miraculous supply of food before he sent them back to their homes that evening. It was a dramatic snapshot of the Good Shepherd providing nourishment for his sheep, not just spiritual nourishment, but food for their bodies as well.

The pain and suffering adults experience is endless and varied. They not only carry pain left over from childhood, but new adverse experiences seem never to end, which further complicate their lives. Whether a person is single or married, or a vowed religious, it makes no difference; pain and suffering are the heritage of all of us.

Being in a religious community brings its own problems. You are alone with other monks or friars who basically are strangers. To a certain extent it is similar to being in the military. You not only work with strangers, you live with them. They come from all kinds of backgrounds and cultures. You are fundamentally alone. Some you may feel comfortable with and they may become friends; others you never can become close to, and it is not easy to even trust them. Relationships are painfully complicated, because everyone is related in different ways to different people, which multiplics the various involvements of each in so many complex and tangled relationships. Some are open and innocent and suffer from the insensitivity of those who never seem to be aware of others' needs. Some are quiet and detached, and it is difficult to know what they are thinking; some are gossips, and these can never be trusted, yet they are your brothers, or sisters, in your religious family, and you must be charitable toward them. Ultimately, for your own safety, you find yourself very much alone, unable to share deeply with anyone. That is one of the great burdens of religious life, and it is that very aloneness that can propel a religious toward a deeper intimacy with God and lead a religious to what he or she should be, an intimate of God's presence, learning to live with God.

Besides the complicated relationships in religious life there are the petty jealousies and other strange feelings that lie beneath the surface of individuals and manifest themselves in ways that can be hurtful and sometimes destructive. When reading the lives of the monastic saints, you can see how difficult their lives were in the monasteries and how much they suffered. Yet it was that suffering itself that help to fashion them into the great saints they finally became. And again, it was their own intimacy with the Good Shepherd and the delicate work of the Holy Spirit that molded them into the beautiful images of Jesus that made them the inspiration to millions for centuries to come.

I don't mean to give the impression that religious life is all suffering. It is a beautiful life, and even to this day I feel the tug at my heart to go back to the monastery, because of the joy and peace and intimacy with God I experienced, in spite of the difficulties.

Married life, on the other hand, though a beautiful calling from God, is a very difficult vocation, with complications all its own. It is a way of life that demands an understanding of human nature for which practically no married couples, especially when they become parents, are ever prepared. The early years of marriage are often blissful and filled with hope, and even though the couple are deeply in love and caring of one another, it is not easy to adjust to each other's differences in personality, and family backgrounds, and spiritual values. These differences and the difficulties in making the necessary adjustments soon show that, even though married love offers the greatest human joy we can experience here on earth, it is fragile and never easy to nurture in a way that assures its steady growth and permanence. Its fragile nature is fraught with unforeseeable situations that arise as differences in personal feelings, values, and attitudes emerge.

Even though there are many inspiring married couples, there are also others whose relationships border on nightmares. If a priest or minister is particularly adept at counseling, he or she will have a counseling workload that for a psychiatrist would be a full-time job. I could often see trouble on the horizon even before the marriage took place, especially if one or both had a serious problem with alcohol, drugs, anger, or just plain selfishness. Years later I was still trying to help some of these couples.

Alcoholism is one of the most serious problems in a marriage. The reasons for this disease are many. The effects are devastating. They affect not only the relationship between the husband and wife but also affect the children. No child likes to see a parent drunk every night, or even on occasion. It destroys the healthy image the child needs to have of a parent. Drinking also wears on the intimacy of the love relationship between the husband and wife. There are few things that undermine the enjoyment of sex as much as a drunk.

One woman finally reached a point where she couldn't take it any more. She called me and told me of her decision, and asked if I would talk to her husband. She told me he finally agreed to meet with me. When he came to the rectory, I let him do a lot of the talking. Of course, he told me he thought his wife didn't love him, and it was humiliating for him. "Yes, I drink, and I admit, I'm mean sometimes, but it's because of the way she treats me."

"How does she treat you?"

"As if I'm a total stranger in my own house. I give her everything she wants. I don't know what more I can do for her."

"Do you ever tell her you love her?"

"That's only words. You show love by actions."

"Like hitting her, or making love to her when you're drunk?"

"C'mon, Father, she knows I love her."

"How could she know?"

"I work hard, and there isn't anything I wouldn't do for her."

"I know you're a good man, have an excellent reputation in the community, and are a good father."

"I love my kids, Father."

"You spend a lot of time with them?"

"No, that's the mother's job."

"Do the kids know you love them?"

"I'm sure they do."

"How do you know? Do they tell you they love you?"

"No, and that bothers me, because they tell their mother they love her, but they never tell me."

"Doesn't that say something? Doesn't it bother you that they don't tell you? It is obvious that it's important to you that your kids tell you that they love you. Don't you think it might also important to your wife and kids? Don't you think your wife needs to hear that you appreciate all the things she does for you and for your kids? I'm sure you like to hear your boss at work tell you when you have done a good job. It makes you realize that she notices the good work you do. But, then, you're a tough man. Maybe you don't need that kind of stuff. After all, it's only words."

"You can't change the way you were brought up, Father. And that's the way I was brought up."

"Tony, I know you are a good man, and you have always been there when I needed you to do things around the parish, and I am sure you have the potential for being a wonderful husband and father, so it is not for me to criticize you. But if you value your marriage and your children's love and respect, you might want to do a little soul searching."

"Well, I'm glad I could tell you my side of the story. I got it off my chest. My wife was right. She said you're easy to talk to, but why do your soft words hurt so much?"

Tony was a good man, though I don't think he was the kind that felt he needed God, but in spite of the problems the couple were having, it was clear that God was very present to that family and was working quietly in each of them. The important thing was, even though there were rough spots, they cared for one another. Their three beautiful young children, who were very caring, said a lot about the basic attitudes of the parents, in spite of serious shortcomings.

Of course, it is not always the husband who is at fault. Wives can also be abusive, in ways that might not be apparent. Women are naturally more sensitive and refined than most men. They take better care of their looks and their appearances. Men are frequently not that concerned about those things. It might be nothing for a man to wear the same shirt two or three days in a row. I heard a wife saying to her husband one day, "When are you going to change that shirt? It stinks. You're such a slob." I could tell the fellow was embarrassed, especially since she said it in front of me. To him it was a real put-down.

And often if a wife is better educated than her husband, it is difficult and embarrassing when he uses bad grammar, or mispronounces words, or is ignorant of so many things going on in the world. It can be very humiliating for a man if, in her own embarrassment over his ignorance, she tells him in front of others that he doesn't know what he's talking about, or if she tells him before they arrive as guests at a party not to talk much or "the other guests will see how ignorant you are." In many marriages, this is ordinary daily fare. Often men put up with it, realizing that it may be true, but it is still abusive and demeaning. These are just examples, but the variety of this kind of abuse can be limitless and over time can slowly wear down a relationship by undermining the tender feelings a couple should have for each other. The strange thing about this kind of behavior is that many women don't even realize they are being abusive.

A particularly painful experience in marriage involves attitudes toward sexual relations. Women need love making to be an expression of tenderness and caring as well as a physical expression of love. Men often seem to care only about the physical sensations of making love; once they are satisfied, it's over for them, even though the wife is just beginning to respond. That is so crude. I was always horrified when I was told about things like this and that a husband never told his wife he loved her or expressed anything tender when they were making love.

On the other hand, I was shocked to hear how often wives make their husbands feel they are doing them a favor when they allow them to make love. That has to be humiliating. Marriage relationships can be such a beautiful expression of human joy, and a source of comfort, and the intimacy a time of great satisfying joy in the tenderness they feel for each other. Unfortunately, only too often relationships in marriage are a cause of deep emotional pain and suffering. Over time, thoughtlessness and lack of caring can destroy the relationship to the point where there is nothing left but routine behavior, devoid of feeling and compassion. I have found that one powerful means of restoring the beauty of their original tenderness is for a couple to kneel down at the bedside at night, hold hands, and pray together, talking honestly to God about each other. This can awaken their realization of how much they really do mean to each other and how they have failed to express their need and love for each other. Awareness of God's presence in their lives brings a whole new dimension into the relationship, and in time that awareness can help them to realize that they have a responsibility before God to care for each other and help each other to grow not only in happiness but also in holiness. That is the first step in developing a mature relationship.

The most painful experience in a family is the death of a child. I don't think parents can ever experience pain worse than losing a son or daughter. There seems to be no logical reason for a child to die before he or she has even begun to find some fulfillment in life. When a tragedy like this happens, it is the worst test of faith for a mother and father to undergo. They ask themselves why it happened for years to come. And there is no answer, just the gnawing, painful wonder if God really cares. Though faith is frequently tested in such a loss, it is also an experience that often leads to a deeper intimacy with God and ultimately to the realization that their child was a special child who had a mission to accomplish, usually involving the lives of others, and when that mission was accomplished God took that young person home.

Strangely enough, I have seen the lives of parents who have lost a child, whether in infancy or adolescence or young adult years, become more mature spiritually and with a deeper compassion and understanding of the pain and hardship in other people's lives. At the same time, they have come to a realization that God taking a child to heaven is not an evil, but, in God's eyes, a gift and a special blessing to the child.

Recently, my Aunt Florence died at ninety-one. She was my mother's younger sister, had been married, had three children and a devoted husband. My first memories of her were when she was a teenager, a bobby-soxer, way back in those days. She was a happy girl and full of fun. Her adult life, however, was filled with sorrow. Her son, Richard, died of cancer in his twenties, leaving a wife and young son. The parents were devastated. Later, one of the daughters, who was only in her thirties, died of cancer. It is painful enough for parents to lose one child, but then a second one pushes the grief beyond imagining. Then Florence's husband died, and not long after, Sondra, her remaining daughter, who had been a public-health nurse and a powerful activist prodding the medical officials to provide vaccines and medicines for children, became ill with cancer. This horrible disease spread slowly over the next few years through her whole body, and then she too died. Florence had seen her just the day before. Then when she received the news that Sondra had died, Florence herself died within a few hours. She had lived to see each of her children die. I cannot even begin to comprehend the terrible pain that woman must have suffered. Parents don't expect a child to die before them. But to lose all of their children is beyond comprehension.

What always amazed me whenever I went to see Aunt Florence was her cheerfulness and her steel-like strength of personality. It was the signature of what she was, and it came from an undying attachment to her faith and the intimacy of her life with Jesus, who was always real to her. She would tell me she could not have survived if it had not been for the closeness of Jesus and his mother in her life. Those relationships were real to her and were the cause of her happy, cheerful spirit in spite of not just the painful memories, but all the physical pain she was undergoing the last few years of her life, when her body would not accept pain killers. She is for me a powerful example of the ability to rise above the most horrible suffering of body and spirit and still find peace, and even joy, in the midst of it all.

5

Suffering in the Workplace

The workplace takes up a big chunk of time in our lives, and we want it to be a pleasant experience. Often it is. Many people enjoy their work immensely. There are also many, however, for whom work, and the atmosphere surrounding it, is a daytime nightmare. Relationships are what define the atmosphere where people spend this great part of their lives. Those relationships are complicated. First, there is the relationship between the employer and the employees, and vice versa. In a small workplace that relationship is more personal and can be either pleasant or difficult. A woman in her forties came to talk to me one day about the problem she was having at work. She was on the verge of tears.

"What happened?" I asked her.

"I've been working at my job for over twenty years, and my boss has never said one nice thing about how I do my work. I put everything into what I do and try to do it perfectly. And I think I do a good job, but he never once has given me the satisfaction of letting me know that I do good work."

"Has he ever said anything negative or criticized your work for any reason?"

"No."

"Then I think you can assume that he's happy with your work."

"But can't he tell me once in a while?"

"Unfortunately, there are some people who are stingy with their praise, even if they know the person's work is outstanding. Often it's the way they have been brought up. It's too bad they have to be that way, and it is stressful to have to work with that kind of a person. You are fortunate that he doesn't find fault with your work. That kind of personality can be very critical in pointing out people's mistakes but never offer praise for a job well done."

"But there's one girl who works with us that he praises all the time."

"Well, that can be a problem for you. There can be any number of reasons why he treats some people one way treats others differently. Perhaps he has a liking for that person, and even if she doesn't do as good a job as you, he might still praise her because he likes her. Who knows? I have a boss myself. And he called me into his office only four times, and each time to complain about someone's complaint about me. I know I do good work and in all the time I have been working, never once did he tell me I did a good job. So, you see, that mentality is common. Sometimes such persons are jealous or may be preoccupied with the way their boss feels about them."

"But if I am going to continue working in this place, I have to feel comfortable," the woman finally stated.

"That's important. And I think the best way to feel comfortable is to build up your own confidence in yourself. You know you do a good job. Don't do it to please him. When you go to work, talk to God about it, and tell him that you are going to do this work for him, that you know that God is pleased with whatever you do for him. Everything we do, we should do for God. He is our Boss. We work and live for him. Every little thing we do for him, he appreciates. So, if you can get used to working like that, and keep your mind focused on that, your work, even in an atmosphere that is otherwise unpleasant, can be turned into a way of pleasing God, because he is there with you and you know he appreciates what you are doing for him."

"I'll try it."

"Good."

Not every unpleasant situation in a place of work is that easy to resolve. Some situations are a living version of hell, where personnel do not get along, can't stand each other, and all day, every day do nothing but find fault with each other. Some are gossips and can't be trusted. Some are just downright mean. Others have problems at home, and they bring the misery to work with them.

What has always amazed me is that some people who have lived under circumstances like this not only tolerate it but are not even bothered by it. That takes a very special kind of person. I asked a lady once who was a victim of circumstances like this why it never seems to bother her. "Oh, it's simple, Father, I know who I am, and I know I'm good. If those nasty creeps want to be like that, I'll be damned if I'll let myself become the receptacle for their bitterness. If they think they are going to transfer their meanness to me, I just won't let them. That makes them even more upset. But if that's the way they want to be, that's their problem. I learned that from Jesus' example with the Pharisees. They hated him, yet he never gave them the satisfaction that they were getting through to him, and that drove them crazy. The bottom line was, he knew they had problems, and he was not going to let them dump their misery on him. So, they walked away even more upset. I have a good teacher. I guess that's the way we have to be. Have enough confidence in who we are and if people want to be miserable, don't let them dump their misery on us. It's Jesus' secret to inner peace, though he expressed it a little more diplomatically by saying that we should always forgive."

Forgiveness, in all circumstances, is always the end of suffering.

We don't forgive because somebody hurt us and we pretend they didn't. We realize that we live and move and have our being not in the workplace but in God. The hurt never really happened at all. God is Love, so Love is where we really are, whether we know it or not. The secret to peace is to know it.

6

Suffering from Injuries
and Illness

About a year and a half ago, while cutting down a large tree, and carting away the logs and long branches, I damaged a disk in my back that impinged on the sciatic nerve. At first the pain was not too bad, but as time went on, it grew worse, so much worse that it was unbearable. In the past I could always stand pain; once when I crushed a disk in my back and withstood the pain for four months before going to the hospital to have an operation. That pain I could bear. The pain this time was not only unbearable, but it was doing things to me that were literally changing my personality.

I could not sleep. I could not stand or sit, or lie down, or kneel. I could not put my socks on or tie my shoes, and I was alone. After two weeks of the most excruciating pain, I was totally unable to function. I had no interest in writing. I did not want to see people, though I managed to force myself to be gracious when people came to talk with me. I cooked only what little I felt like eating. I was beginning to have terrible feelings of bad self-esteem and the self-image of a person who was totally useless. At night I was prone to horrible panic attacks and feelings that I was losing my mind. One of the medicines triggered hallucinations. I was beginning to understand what so many people go through in their lives, and I then began to realize that God was allowing this because this was an area in my life experiences that was missing. I had always had a very strong will and could surmount any kind of pain or obstacle I had to face, which made it difficult for me to understand others who may not have my kind of mental or psychological toughness.

But now I had come face to face with a pain that could drive a person not only to insanity but to suicide. This I could never understand before. I needed to know if I was just exaggerating my pain or if I was right in the way I felt. I called a friend who had worked in a hospital in Florida and asked her what sciatic pain was like, as she had had it for six months. She told me that sciatic pain could easily drive a person to insanity and even suicide.

Now I could finally identify with people who live lives that they find impossible to manage. I could see how they desperately needed God and a healing from God. For a clergyperson to put further demands on a person hurting like this before allowing that person to come close to God would only drive that person away from God. I saw in an only too vivid way how cruel and callous such treatment is, and yet it is not rare among some clergy who do not appreciate the pain in people's lives. This is what made the Good Shepherd so different from the scribes and Pharisees. He saw people's pain and its debilitating effect on their lives; the scribes and Pharisees saw only violations of the Law. We clergy must rise above that mentality and develop the heart of the Good Shepherd, so we can bring his healing love to the suffering sheep. I was becoming more and more convinced that our role as priests is not to be judges of people's morality or spiritual condition or to be moral policemen, but to be good shepherds, called by God to heal the destructive pain of God's children.

Then I thought of my godson Joey, who, when he was in the depths of his cocaine addiction, and living in a hell of anguish, was fortunately still able to relate to Jesus, as he had since his childhood, and found a church that was open all day. He would go there after classes at Juilliard and spend hours before the Blessed Sacrament talking to Jesus, pouring his heart out to him for help. At a time when he was in the depths of shame and on the verge of despair, he clung to Jesus, his friend from infancy. He never let anything or anyone keep him from communion when he went to mass. No one could keep him from Jesus, and after three horrible years for all of us, God finally freed him from his addiction, and then called him home. Joey found his only comfort in his beautiful and extraordinary friendship with Jesus, which was truly his salvation.

My own experience of that excruciating sciatic pain that was so debilitating was a lesson I needed to learn so I could understand the lives of people who endure unbelievable suffering and impossible torment and be able to help them when they came to me. For many people pain is not just occasional, but day and night every day with no reprieve. Fortunately, in my situation, after a week of tests and experimenting with various combinations of medications, the doctors finally relieved the pain, so for the past year I have had only a bearable numbness in the lower part of my left leg.

What I gained in that lesson was an understanding of catastrophic pain and its effect on people's lives, especially on their spiritual lives. Suffering is indeed a mystery, and my knowledge was and still is too shallow to plumb its depths. I am learning more and understanding more deeply as I write about the many things that people have shared with me over the years about their own difficult lives.

Many years ago I did get a brief glimpse of the mystery of suffering and God's intimacy with people who suffer. I took my mother to visit her lifelong friend in a nursing home in California. Anna had been my mother's friend since childhood. Anna had rheumatoid arthritis as a child, and as she got older, she would develop terrible cases of psoriasis, which necessitated her being hospitalized. Her body suffered unbearable pain when anybody touched her, but the nurses had to change her sheets every day to dispose of the scales that fell off her body. When Anna was sixteen, her legs had become so deformed that the doctors had to break them to straighten them out.

Later my mother's favorite brother married Anna, who was a beautiful woman. But after she got pregnant, they moved to California, and later on her husband left her. Now she had to fend for herself and her child. She and my mother corresponded faithfully for thirty-five years. Knowing how close they were, I decided to surprise my mother one summer when we went on vacation. When she asked me where we were going this particular year, I told her California. When we arrived there, we first visited some friends, then I quietly drove to Anna's nursing home. When I stopped, my mother asked me why we were stopping there. I told her, "I have a little surprise for you."

We went inside, and I asked the nurse where Anna was, and she showed us the ward. When we went in, there were only a few beds occupied in a ward with at least twenty beds. As we approached Anna's bed, Anna looked at us and said, "Margaret? Joseph?" She was so surprised to see us, and although she had not seen me since I was a baby, she recognized us immediately.

When my mother saw the condition Anna was in, with arthritic deposits that made each hand look as if it had ten fingers, and all deformed, and her knees folded up, and her arms deformed, my mother started to cry.

Anna said to her: "Margaret, I hope you are not crying for me. I have to be the happiest person in the world. God is always so close to me. If you only knew how close God is to me all the time!"

Then I started to cry. The nurse had told us before we went in that Anna was in intense pain day and night and had been for years, yet she never complained and always had a smile. She was not able to move her body; all her joints were frozen, and the nurses had to turn her carefully around to change her position every hour to help her feel comfortable. To see that woman in constant agony and to hear her say that she had to be the happiest person in the world was something I could not understand. That, I think, was my introduction to the mystery of pain and its identifying relationship with the suffering Jesus. All I could think of was Saint Paul's words about making up in our own bodies for the sufferings that are lacking in Christ. What did that mean? I could never imagine anything lacking in Christ, and I assumed that was part of the mystery. Eventually, what Saint Paul said made sense, when I realized we are baptized into Jesus and become members of his mystical body, of which he is the head. So, as members of his body we also must play our role in helping Jesus save souls by our suffering on the cross with him. Anna brought to the forefront of my consciousness the issue of unbearable pain and its mystical relationship with Jesus. I thought about what she had said and what it meant so many times. With no other being could a suffering person be brought into intimate contact, or so mystically bonded, as with Jesus.

As Jesus became incarnate in Mary's womb, he literally becomes intimately present in the soul of a suffering person who is open to welcoming him, and that presence makes it possible in time to override the pain and experience an incomprehensible joy and peace. This was a pivot around which I could from then on contemplate the reality of human pain and the suffering victim's intimacy with the suffering Jesus. That phenomenon is unique in the human experience and made me realize that Jesus is not an option in human destiny. He is the only being who can give meaning to human life. He alone, whether we desire it or not, or are aware or not, or want him or not, is still an intimate part of each of our lives and gives meaning to each of us, precisely because he is the God who made us. Thinking about his relationship with Anna, I learned to appreciate just what it means to believe that Jesus is an intimate friend and presence to each of us, even to those of us who choose to ignore or reject him all through life. I am becoming convinced that each of us, whether we have faith or different faith, or no faith, at some time has to deal with the reality of Jesus in our life. How we respond to that is personal and is between ourselves and God. Even if we do not know Jesus, Jesus, being God, is still the reality that relates to each one of us in the depths of our soul, and without realizing it, when we are touched by God, it is the divine person of Jesus who is within us and who is calling us into intimacy with him. "I will not leave you orphans. I will come and live within you, and be with you always." This is what he promised before he returned to heaven, where suffering is not even a word.

When we were leaving Anna's bedside, it was painful for all of us, as we know it would be the last time we would see her in this life. Leaving her meant that this poor but blessed soul was totally alone in the world, in an almost empty room where all she had was God and the caring strangers who loved her and were inspired by her as they cared for her day and night. Also seeing the tortured condition of Anna's deformed fingers, I wondered how she could have written letters with such precise script when her fingers could hardly move and were in such pain. As we were leaving, we tried to hold back our tears until we were out of Anna's presence, but it was impossible. My poor mother, I think, would have liked to stay there to be a comfort to her.

The experience of Anna's illness and her faith was impossible for me to understand, but it started me on a lifelong search for a mystical meaning to human suffering and made me often ponder the meaning of those cryptic words of Saint Paul: "In my own flesh I fill up what is lacking in the sufferings of Christ for the sake of his body, the church" (Col 1:24).

Yes, I knew intellectually that the sufferings of this brave woman were in some way tied and identified with the sufferings of Jesus. How else explain her joyful intimacy with the divine presence within her? Those words of Saint Paul I was to consider for years to come, determined to understand as fully as I could what they meant. I could not comprehend how Jesus' sufferings could be in any way lacking. Were not his sufferings sufficient for the salvation of us all? He alone is our Redeemer. If some people are reluctant to refer to the Blessed Mother as co-redemptrix of the human race, how can Saint Paul tacitly give us the same, though diminished function when we suffer. With Mary it is understandable. She chose to bring our Redeemer into the world, and to that extent the title of co-redemptrix

has certain limited meaning. But it is hard to see
that our sufferings can merit such distinction. Yet,
it seems clear that as members of Jesus' mystical
body, in our sufferings we share with Jesus his
role in saving people, even though our role is so
insignificant by comparison. But it does emphasize
the importance Jesus places on our intimacy with
him when we do suffer. He is very much present
with us during these difficult times, ever strength-
ening, comforting, helping us to understand our
closeness to him at such times and how valuable
our sufferings are in helping other souls to receive
God's grace.

It is the love of Jesus that endows our humble
contribution with spiritual value by making us
members of his body. This incorporation into Jesus
is a mystery unique to Jesus and his family, which
he called his church, and bonds us to him in a
union that is more intimate than the bond between
body and soul. So, when we suffer, it is bound up
with Jesus' redemptive sufferings on Calvary, as
there is no past or future with God. All is present,
even the process of his ongoing redemption of us
all, so our lives today were present to Jesus at that
time. So, strangely, we can still be present with
Jesus on Calvary in spite of the difference in time,
because to God all things are present. We can suffer
with him as he is suffering regardless of the vast
distance in time. And in the end we are never closer
to Jesus than when we are crucified with him in our
own personal suffering. And, even though suffering
is in one sense an evil, Jesus did not take it away,

because without suffering we cannot grow. So he did something better: he transformed suffering into a treasure. A piece of coal and a diamond are made of the same substance, carbon, but when a piece of coal suffers by being subjected to the intense pressures and heat of the earth, in time all the impurities are driven out of it and it is transformed into a priceless diamond. And that is what God does with us, as we are being transformed into something that resembles the divine presence living within us.

As good shepherds, we also need to know that some illnesses that are difficult for many people to understand are an added burden to those who suffer from them. AIDS, mental illnesses, and illnesses that severely affect the victims' appearance have a profound effect on persons afflicted with them. Often they feel that they are the modern lepers in society and find it difficult not to believe that they are spurned and rejected by others and by society in general. Even relatives of such persons can have a difficult time with them, not because they reject them, but because they do not know how to socialize with them for fear they may appear to be patronizing or just do not know what to say. When there are attempts to socialize, there are long pauses in the conversations and the visits end up being very uncomfortable and, as a result, less frequent. Those who live with them share the burden, often with only a few friends to comfort them.

As a result people afflicted with these illnesses are very much alone and feel a horrible sense of loneliness and abandonment, often abandonment by God, with the question haunting them, "Why would God let this happen to me if he really cares for me and loves me?"

Among the most shameful aspects of ordinarily good people's attitude about people who suffer from diseases like AIDS are the baseless and harsh judgments they make, often in the presence of the victims themselves, making remarks like, "It's God's punishment for their unhealthy lifestyle," and "It's their own fault. They have free will and they made their choice; now let them live with it." Not only are these judgments heartless, but they are totally out of place on the lips and in the heart of a Christian.

From my associations with people suffering from these illnesses, I found them to be authentically spiritual. When I tended them in the hospital I was impressed with their patient and humble acceptance of the agony they were undergoing and the tender intimacy they manifested in their relationship with Jesus. They could be beautiful examples for others of how to die humbly and with dignity as they realize that in so short a time they will be with God. I think God manifests a unique tenderness toward these people when they are ill and dying, even though many so-called nice people hold them in low esteem.

Each of these suffering children of God wears the face of Christ in a unique way. The best way for us to be good to them is to see it.

It used to be cancer that was the illness that dared not speak its name. Then it was AIDS. Now it is Alzheimer's disease.

It scares us and seems to creep up on all of us. As we grow older, we tire easily and push ourselves to work harder when we don't have the energy or the strength. It is then that we become aware of our previously untapped and infrequently used willpower. Our memories play games on us and we can't even remember what we went upstairs for or into the kitchen to get what we so urgently needed just thirty seconds ago. For the first few weeks it doesn't bother us, and we can even laugh when we tell family members how funny it was. But as time goes on, we no longer find it funny and we don't dare share it with others for fear they will start looking at us strangely or hint that we might consider a nursing home. Then we find ourselves forgetting people, places, and things that we were familiar with all our life. The names of best friends slip our mind at most strategic times.

For some, this process of memory loss is within acceptable limits, but for others it progressively becomes frightening. Not only do we forget why we went into another room to get something, but we forget where things are in the house. In time we find ourselves not recognizing old friends and family members we haven't seen in a long time. One morning we wake up and don't recognize the person lying next to us in bed. That is painful and bewildering.

It is painful for the person's spouse or family member as well. You still love the person, but he or she is becoming what author Bob Betterton describes in the title of his book as "the familiar stranger who lives in our house." The only recourse sometimes is just to be normal and act as if what is said makes sense and meet needs as they present themselves. Even though loved ones sometimes won't know exactly who you are, you know *for* them that they are really whole, and that is a healing knowledge for both of you. My friend Mike, who has been caring for his beloved wife for ten years, tells me: "You can't take it seriously. That would kill both of you. It is what it is. You go on. Some people spend their whole lives and go to seminars and pay big bucks trying to live in 'the present moment.' A person with advanced Alzheimer's knows *only* the present moment. So I live on Vickie's clock. That's hardly the worst thing in the world."

Eventually, the situation may reach the point where the person is so unaware it is not safe to leave him or her alone; twenty-four-hour care is necessary, either at home or somewhere else. The painful decision of having to place someone you love so deeply into a nursing home where there will be appropriate care day and night can haunt you. At that point you may experience emotional and psychological suffering that is almost unbearable. You cannot just go on with your life and forget the person who has forgotten you. That is unthinkable.

Another dear friend, an army general, placed his wife in a nursing home and afterward never missed a day visiting her, even though she didn't recognize him. A fellow officer one day asked him why he visits his wife every day when she doesn't even know who he is. My friend's response: "But I know who *she* is. She is my wife, and I love her, and even though she may not know me, she at least knows she has a friend who comes to visit her every day and makes her happy. And when we meet again, she will remind me of all the times I came to visit her in the nursing home. She will know then how loyal I was to her."

That takes not only love and loyalty but great faith, faith in Jesus' promise that one day all our sufferings will end and we will be together again in another and happier place. The beginning of the end of suffering is indeed to live and love moment by moment.

7

Suffering from Loneliness

One of the most common aches in the human heart is loneliness; it may be the most prevalent illness in the world. It is not found only in people who live alone, isolated from others, even their nearest neighbors. One would be surprised, watching the hordes of people in Times Square in New York on New Year's Eve, that in that vast crowd there are thousands suffering from debilitating loneliness and may go there perhaps to escape from their frightening solitude only to find out that there is no escape, only a temporary respite.

I never understood loneliness and the effect it has on the disintegration of the human psyche and the personality itself. I had experienced loneliness only once, and it was such a frightening experience, I was fortunately able to avoid it all the rest of my life until recently, when I was in that terrible sciatic pain. When I was fourteen years old I entered the seminary. At Christmas we were allowed go home for three weeks. At the end of the vacation, I returned and arrived at the campus at two in the afternoon. It had been snowing all day and when I got out of the taxi, I saw that none of the driveways had been plowed and the snow was over a foot

103

deep. It was like the place had been abandoned, as it really was, for three weeks. There was not one footprint in the snow. The quiet was so eerie, I could almost hear the snowflakes falling. There was not the slightest noise or sound of any kind. I had never felt so alone. All I could think of was an empty planet. I had no cell phone or anything like these modern necessities. I was trapped in three hundred acres totally devoid of life.

I went into the chapel to see if one of the priests might be there. It was empty. I prayed, went outside, and seeing my own footprints in the snow gave me an odd feeling. I yelled, "Anybody around?" No response. I opened the door to the dormitory. Still not a sound. All of a sudden the most horrible feeling of homesickness overwhelmed me. I had never experienced such a frightening phenomenon together with the panic and anxiety that accompanied it. I was all alone on an empty planet in outer space. That thought seemed like reality, and it seized me. "I was so happy at home. Why did I have to leave?" I never realized how alone I was in this place, even when the others come, they are all strangers, and I mean nothing to anyone here. Its force frightened me, and I realized if I gave in to it, it could ruin my life, because I knew this is where I was supposed to be. I had known that from my childhood, and I could not allow my feelings to affect me and drive me off course. My father had drilled into us, "Never let your emotions tell you what to do. Do what you know you are supposed to do. Live on principles and follow your reason, not your feelings. They are blind and will lead you astray." I had heard that so many times. This turned out to be my first big chance to practice it. Fortunately, about an hour later the other seminarians started filing in, and after a few hours the horrible feeling dissolved. I will never forget the feeling, though, and forever realized how destructive it could be and the effect it must have on a person who could not shake it.

It was not until many years later that I came face to face with a person who was totally wrapped in loneliness. I was a pastor at the time. I got a phone call from a man who asked if I could hear his confession. I told him he could come over anytime he wanted. He said it was impossible for him to leave his house and asked if I could please come over to his house to hear his confession. I told him I would be there in a few minutes.

When I arrived at the rather ill-kept rooming house and went to his apartment, I knocked. When the door opened, I saw the most frightening figure standing before me. He had no face. I panicked, and smiled hello, as if he just looked normal, and gave him a hug as I give everybody. I tried to identify a mouth, but it was not well formed. There seemed to be no ears. The man could see through two tiny slits. He had no hair. He was gracious and offered me a seat, and we sat and talked briefly. He was so grateful I came. Then he made his confession, and I prayed and called down Jesus' forgiveness for whatever sins the poor man had ever committed. I left shortly afterward.

He called again the next day, and I went over to his room again, and two days later he called again, and I tried to tell him that he really didn't need confession, that he was one of the holiest people I had ever met. I tried to assure him that he was very close to God. He said he needed the grace of confession to keep him from committing suicide. I did not believe that that was true, so again telling him that he had no sins to confess, we talked for a while, and when the conversation ended, I hung up. Later that day it came over the news that he had committed suicide. I felt terrible, but I did not know what else I could have done. When others in the past had called and told me they were about to commit suicide, I acted quickly and made sure the police or some family member was aware and went to the house. With this man, I felt he had been dealing with his horrible situation and had been coping with it so far. So I did nothing. I later found out that he had been severely burned in a fire. The flesh on his face had melted. He did have a family, and his wife visited him, but she did not want the children to see him in such a condition for fear of the horrible emotional effect it might have on them. It was then that I realized the depths of the man's total loneliness, a loneliness that really did ultimately end in his death. It became clear that the man was alone, unable to see his children and his friends. He felt totally abandoned and devoid of human companionship and human love. From that day on, loneliness took on an entirely new meaning for me and added to my understanding of the kinds of pain people were suffering. I realized also for the first time that love is just as necessary for life as breathing. It seemed every day more and more people came, sharing with me their painful burdens, all different, and so many of them devastating, without any possibility of a cure or emotional healing. Some of those who came were children. I began to understand Jesus' exposure to human suffering and what the title good shepherd meant to him.

Since I retired and wrote *Joshua*, I have had to travel to various countries and most states in my own country. On one trip I went to Haiti. As soon as we entered the city, men surrounded the car with their hands out, "Please, please."

It broke my heart to see so many grown men reduced to such degradation. I looked at them with compassion but knew I could do nothing. When the taxi passed, I broke down and cried. I could not bear the thought of such soul-filled pain.

Everyplace I went, not just in Haiti, I was surrounded by suffering people. It was not that only suffering people came to my talks; but yes, I guess it was true, maybe only the suffering did come to my talks. Very few ever told me that life was a most enjoyable experience, though some rare few did tell me that they could not understand my dismay at seeing so much pain and anguish, especially in people's experience with their religion. Fortunately, there were some who up to that point in their lives had been spared tragedy and unusual pain or suffering of any kind, and they found it odd that I knew so many people who had bad experiences with their religion.

However, there were many who could not wait to pour out their souls, telling me the tragedies that they or their family members had suffered. Many told me of the guilt they felt because they were mad at God for having put such heavy burdens on their lives and because, in their anger against God, they had left the church to show their resentment. There were many who told me stories of how mean and insensitive clergy were toward them. Those sad tales I really did not enjoy hearing, as I had my own pain that I was carrying over similar issues with bishops and clergy. But it was good that people felt comfortable enough to bare their souls and tell me about their own hurt in the church, so I listened and said as little as I could so as not to invalidate their experiences. It was also a rich learning experience for me. It taught me about the terrible pain and anguish some people carry all their lives.

After loneliness, I think guilt is probably the worst ache in the human heart. Like a cancer it infects the very soul of a person and severely erodes healthy self-love. If the guilt is severe, it can in time destroy a person. Even the best of people make decisions that at the time seem right or unavoidable; other options may not be available to them. Then they feel guilt for something that they had little control over, and they feel the pain deeply, precisely because they are good people. This is so common. Saint Peter's denial of Jesus is a good example of that. He loved Jesus with his whole being, yet in his weakness and uncontrollable fear, he could not own up to his friendship with Jesus. Yet, he was still Jesus' close friend, and Jesus knew that his love was real, but Jesus also knew that Peter was weak. It was the shame, and humility that flowed from that shame, that became the foundation of Peter's strength and heroism later on. Never again would he depend solely on his own human strength; rather, he trusted in the grace and strength of God to guide him and be his source of courage. Eventually, he would make the ultimate witness to Jesus by his own crucifixion, upside down.

What made the pain worse not just for Peter, but for Jesus as well, was the fact that while Peter was cursing and swearing his denial of Jesus, it was in earshot of Jesus inside the high priest's palace where Jesus was being interrogated. They could all hear Peter cursing and swearing his disloyalty to his Master. When Jesus was then led out into the courtyard and passed Peter, he looked at Peter and Peter remembered the words of Jesus earlier—"Before the cock crows, you will deny me three times." Peter then went out and wept bitterly.

One of the early fathers of the church wrote that when Peter was growing old, there were furrows carved down his cheeks from the tears he shed every time he remembered the hurt look in Jesus' eyes that night. How does one forget that kind of pain? It remains to the day one dies.

I could go on and on drawing up an extensive catalogue of the kinds of pain and suffering people experience, and after a few pages, not only I, but also the reader, would be depressed. What I would like to be the focus of this manuscript is not an overpowering feeling of the world's pain, but for readers to *recognize* the universal experience of pain and suffering as the lot of us human beings as the important and essential black and purple threads in the tapestry of our life here on earth. Those dark threads in the tapestry give depth and dimension to the masterpiece on the front of the tapestry. Our lives are like tapestries, in which we see only the loose ends as God is weaving the masterpiece on the other side. What we have to do is learn how to approach the dark side of our life and how to handle pain and suffering when our turn comes to experience it.

8

Suffering from Natural Disasters

Who would have dreamed that violent hurricanes would rush along the East Coast of the United States and devastate homes and lives from New Jersey to Connecticut not once but twice in three years? In the twenty-first century the media has reported not one but *three* "storms of the century," the other a vicious nor'easter in this heavily populated area.

I remember when Hurricane Irene slammed into upstate New York early one morning with violent winds coming from the east. The rain lashed horizontally against the front of Joshua House for almost three hours. Then it stopped. Two hours later it started again, but this time the wind was coming from the west and lashed against the back of the house for another two hours, doing the same damage as the first wind, driving up roof shingles and shooting water into the house. Fortuitously, it also scrubbed my front and back windows sparkling clean.

However, a few days later we began to realize that many people in the area were not so fortunate. Clusters of sixty or seventy houses in a low-lying area only a few miles from Joshua House were totally overrun by flooded streams and the Mohawk

River. The foundations buckled and collapsed. Electric wires were destroyed; walls cracked and broke apart. Water in the wells was polluted. The weather was freezing, and most of the people were elderly and had no place to sleep for the night. Who could imagine this in the richest country in the world? What could be done to keep them alive?

Gary, the deacon who works with me, went to visit the place and on his own took on the project of taking care of all these people. Another blessed instrument of the manifestation of the Good Shepherd at work in the lives of people haunted by unexpected natural disaster! Gary worked hard trying to get the remaining people back into their reconditioned homes. Fortunately, the Federal Emergency Management Agency was very efficient in coordinating work projects and asked Gary if he could also help organize a group of people in another area, in Schoharie County, which was also hit hard by the hurricane. Gary talked to the local congressman to try and get funds from Congress to aid in the massive work that had to be done. When the congressman brought up the situation on the floor of the House of Representatives, he was unable to gather any support.

So, Gary, with the help of the diocesan office of Catholic Charities, did all he could to restore the tragic situations back to normal. One of the problems that came up because of the dimensions of the devastation involved the applying of the state building code. The local inspectors felt that there were too many damaged houses in violation of the code, so it was impossible to grant permits to work on the buildings. Gary, not knowing how to resolve that issue, contacted a man in the State Code Department in Albany, who, by coincidence, happened to be Ed Girzone, my brother. Ed had a contact inform the inspectors that in catastrophic situations like this, there were provisions for flexibility in resolving the complex code issues in order to get the people back into their homes. So, one by one, the code issues were resolved, and many of the houses were back in livable condition again.

Another good example of how the Good Shepherd uses local shepherds and others as instruments of God's caring love! It happened during Katrina in New Orleans and during tornadoes throughout the Midwest. During all the violent natural disasters that have been occurring over the past few years, we see on television many examples of heroism on the part of those who sacrifice so much of themselves to help neighbors who have lost family members, especially children and spouses, and everything that they own. Only the heroic love of neighbors was able to save them from almost total despair, showing us graphically that God's love is still alive in those who may live right next door and will rise to the occasion when their love and help is critical.

We cannot understand why God allows natural disasters. Perhaps they are just the normal flow of natural forces. We can understand, and appreciate, that God is always with us in the form of the Good Shepherd, who comes to us whenever there is need. The end of suffering is to become a good shepherd ourselves.

9

Suffering from the Inevitability of Suffering

It has become overwhelmingly clear as I recount memories of the past and all the stories I have listened to that suffering is the lot of human beings on this earth. I know of no one who has escaped it. As my friend Mike Leach says, "No one gets out of this thing alive."

I have known friends who had charmed lives in their younger years and escaped any serious pain only to run headlong into unexpected tragedy as young adults. One lost both parents in an accident. These loving parents were his whole life. When they died, his world fell apart. Just to stay alive was for the longest time almost impossible. He survived only through the help of a compassionate counselor and a man of deep faith who showed him that there was reason to live and that a beautiful future was not only possible but attainable.

Some have experienced suffering even in their tender years. This is something you see quite frequently in the lives of some of the saints. Saint Margaret Mary Alacoque was unwanted by her parents, and they told her so. She was raised by an aunt, who was overbearing and not loving. Her young life was most painful, but it conditioned her for an authentic intimacy with Jesus, who had become her

only comfort. It was that beautiful, mystical relationship with Jesus that became the vehicle for the
inspiration that has touched the lives of millions of
people ever since her death in 1690. The special de-
votion to Jesus that she advocated during her hidden and almost unknown life in the convent is still
extremely popular some four hundred years later.

More recently, a young lady, whose mother left
home when the girl was a child, was left with a
father who had a serious alcoholic problem. In
spite of his debilitating addiction, he tried to be a
good father and give his daughter good principles
and values to live on, and he taught her integrity,
though her life was filled with loneliness and pain.
A grandmother who cared for her was a mother
to her until her death, when the girl was hardly a
teenager. Another horrible heartbreak that made
life for this young girl so much more painful and
lonely! When she married, the marriage did not last,
and the husband's mother was given custody of the
baby. One wonders how much pain a young girl can
take before succumbing to hopelessness.

Years of depression followed, during which unreasonable obstacles made it almost impossible for
her to see her son. Fortunately, a young man who
saw the depth and goodness and high intelligence of
the girl took her under his care and for many years
worked to help her rise from her depression and
near hopelessness. Sometimes, just knowing that
someone loves you and cares for you is a powerful
healing medicine. Also, like Saint Margaret Mary

Alacoque, she found strength and comfort in a tender relationship with Jesus. This gave a whole new meaning to her life, and in spite of continued difficulties she has grown immensely and in a newfound strength has an endurance that seems unshakable.

Eventually, she found a boyfriend and had a child. Shortly after, they separated. Even this did not shake her now strong personality. She told me one day, "If that's the way it has to be, I am glad I found out early. I have my son to care for, and I can't spend my time feeling self-pity." She decided to go to college to get her doctorate in psychology and work with troubled children.

Her whole personality has changed. She is strong and stable, and her little son is a happy child and has the most beautiful love of Jesus. He is the love of her life, and she is so strong, so much at peace, that her whole personality radiates joy and serenity and strength. It is beautiful to see.

In recent years we experienced the tragic holocaust of millions of Jews and Poles and others during the Second World War. Even more recently we all feel the pain of the millions of people in Africa who have been mercilessly raped and slaughtered for no reason other than they belonged to different tribes. And now the wars that are still ongoing and shattering precious lives and dreams bear witness to suffering that is beyond comprehension. The highly respected Rand Corporation, used by the Pentagon for its research, reported recently that of the 1,250,000 American troops that have been in

Iraq and Afghanistan, 310,000 are suffering from serious post-traumatic depression, and another 300,000 from brain damage, to say nothing of the destroyed family relationships and damaged future of the spouses and children of these families. It was also reported that over the past five years there have been over twenty-eight thousand suicides among our troops, a much higher percentage than in any previous war, while politicians boast that they have protected our people from terrorist attacks. One wonders—aren't our troops our people?

Every day we see on television tragedies from natural disasters and cataclysmic occurrences worldwide in which often hundreds of thousands of lives are destroyed or permanently damaged. From all this it is easy to see that suffering and pain are universal. What is so difficult for us to understand is our inability to find a reason for such suffering. All we can say is that it is a frightening phenomenon testifying to a sick and dysfunctional world society. As impossible as it is for us to understand the meaning of all this suffering, it is still critical that we learn to accept the fact of its existence and learn to deal with it in a way that will prevent it from destroying us or crippling us in the living out of our own lives, lives that we must learn to live not just for ourselves but in a way that we can make our own contribution, great or small, to alleviate the suffering of our brothers and sisters around the world, suffering that could be reduced if more people cared enough to do something.

Fortunately, many strong and heroic souls have, by their wisdom, endurance, and limitless patience, taught us ways to understand pain and suffering and, by their example, showed us the way to rise above even the most horrifying personal tragedies and fashion a life that is not only personally productive but an inspiration to others who are struggling with similar seemingly insurmountable suffering. Many of these people through their own suffering have reached out to heal others. What is their source of strength?

Rarely does this strength come from human sources, because from a purely natural point of view suffering is of little value in situations that seem hopeless or purposeless. In practically all the heroic, suffering persons I have met, their strength comes from an intimacy with God that in many instances manifests a strange mystical experience that helps them rise above their pain and find joy in their experience of closeness to God, or an intangible presence in their lives that they cannot define. They know and have the strong conviction that they are not suffering alone. Those with faith draw strength from knowing that God is with them, and Christians feel that their suffering bonds them to the crucified Jesus. They feel that their own suffering helps to save straying souls.

There are so many beautiful persons who have risen above their own personal traumas and each year spend weeks and months traveling to far-away places to help rebuild the lives of the hopeless and destitute. There is a parish in Burke, Virginia, whose pastor suggested to his parishioners that they give up a meal a week during Lent and donate the money saved to help the poor. This parish has a large number of federal government workers as well as people in the military. The first Lent the parish embarked on this program, it collected sixty thousand dollars. With that money a group of parishioners and their pastor went to Haiti and, with the help of the people there, built a number of houses for the poor. It has now been eight years since the parish embarked on this vision, and it has made it a full-time project. The parishioners have collected close to two million dollars and have built many homes as well as a school and other buildings necessary to better the life of the community in Haiti. They also developed a complete pure-water system for the community. The wonderful thing about this group is that they don't think they are doing anything sensational; the parishioners are just thrilled to be able provide a better existence for destitute people struggling to stay alive.

They are following the Good Shepherd, who harkens, sooner or later but surely, to suffering. They inspire us not to wallow in the inevitability of suffering but to enter it and, by entering it, to transform it.

10

Suffering near the End of Life

Jesus assured us, "I will not leave you orphans. I will be with you always." This statement alone expresses Jesus' awareness that our life here on earth is not easy and that we are all afraid of the pain and danger of life's tragedies. Knowing this, Jesus assures us that he is with us, not just Christians, but all of his Father's children all over the world. However, this means little to some people, and has only marginal meaning to most human beings. Even among many people of faith, Jesus is a person far removed from their personal life. Oh, there are many who may believe in him as they were taught from infancy, but as far as looking upon him as a person who really cares enough to be personally and intimately involved in their life, that is not very common, until they find that he is their only resort left, when medicine and doctors fail to help. For the most part we feel that God is far removed from our lives, in another world. We seem to be missing something, and I think part of it is that we view God's kingdom as not quite real, as if it is at the farthest fringes of our universe, and we wonder what God can do anyway.

While pondering this one day, as I was thinking about a friend who had just died, I was wondering

if she was in heaven, and if in heaven, just where is
heaven? It then dawned on me that heaven, God's
dwelling place, is where God is, and since God is everywhere, heaven is everywhere, all around us, just
in another dimension. As Saint Paul wrote, "in him
we live and move and have our being" (Acts 17:28).
If God is everywhere, then heaven is not far away
but is a very real place in that other dimension, so
close that if we could reach through that thin veil
into that dimension, we could touch our loved ones,
whom God has taken home.

God's world moves in and out of our world, and
this is what Jesus meant when he said he would be
with us always. He is ever the same. He is still the
Good Shepherd, just as he was when he was wan-
dering the dusty roads of Palestine, doing the same
thing today among us, without our even realizing it,
reaching out to each of us with his comforting and
healing love, ready and waiting for us to invite him
into our lives so he can befriend us and begin the
healing process that we find so impossible. He has
not stopped doing what he was doing when he was
first on earth. He will always be the Good Shepherd,
touching each of us in the depths of our souls,
healing and protecting us from harm. He is a God
who cares, just as in the days of old. He went about
doing good, mingling among the crowds, always
looking for those who were hurting and lonely and
in need of healing. He is the healing medicine we
need when we are hurting and troubled, but there
are so many who do not or cannot recognize him,
and some, sadly, who refuse to recognize him, so

they miss the comfort of his presence because he will not violate our privacy and intrude unwanted into our lives. He wants us to open our hearts to his presence and his love.

When I was a young boy, not yet a teenager, one of my father's customers in his meat market was the publisher of the important newspaper in Albany, New York. This man dressed with class and was most impressive when he walked so elegantly into my dad's little store.

"Hello, Peter," he would say as he entered.

"Hello, Mr. Jenkins," my father would reply.

"How are you, Peter, and how is the family?"

"Good, thank God."

The man would shake his head and continue, "Peter, why do you always say 'thank God.' God has nothing to do with it. It is your loyalty to your family and your hard work that make you successful."

"Yes, but where would I be without my health, which is always good, thank God."

This exact same exchange repeated itself every week for over thirty-five years. Then the man did not show up for a long time. One day one of the New York State commissioners, who was part of the elite "club" that frequented my Dad's store, told my father, "Peter, your friend has been very sick, in bad shape. You better pray for him."

"I had been wondering about him. I haven't seen him in a long time. I pray for him and all of you every day. We've been together for all these years."

"He needs prayers, Peter. He is not well at all."

A week later Mr. Jenkins came in. He was hardly recognizable. My father could not believe the change. He was but a shadow of a man, and so frail, but still the same exchange took place.

"How are you, Peter, and how is the family?"

"Good, thank God."

"Peter, I finally know what you mean when you say 'thank God.'" That was all he said. He was always a man of few words. He picked up his order and after the two of them said goodbye, the man left. That very week he died. In some way he had an experience of God that in his last moments changed his life. It was no doubt the answer to the prayers of many friends that this man finally found God, though sadly, yet happily, in the last moments of his life.

Holbein's picture of Jesus holding a lighted lantern and knocking at a door for the host to invite him in made me think of this man. Jesus had been knocking at the door of that man's heart all his life, and only in the end did he open the door. The door in this case was the suffering that brought this proud man to humble recognition of the important meaning of that Person who had been knocking at his heart all his life. That One knocking was always there, always present, never giving up, pursuing him until he could resist no longer. He finally opened the door to let this divine Stranger into his life. It was only then that he began to appreciate that divine presence that was always with him, waiting, as a friend and companion, to share his joy, his success, to comfort him in troubled times, and even still more during this his darkest hour, as he was about to leave this world and meet this unknown Friend face to face. The Good Shepherd pursues his lost sheep right to the end.

Another awesome and inspiring story is about my dentist. He and his family had been dear friends of mine for many years. As he grew older he was struck with ALS, often called Lou Gehrig's disease. As the horrible disease progressed, he became weaker and weaker. His muscles rapidly deteriorated. Eventually, he was unable to move his arms and legs and it became impossible for him to walk or even stand up. In time, he found it difficult to swallow food. He could consume only liquids. His caring family had a special contraption for him to lie on and could manipulate it so he was almost standing. Even though it became nearly impossible to eat, talk, or even breathe, we were all inspired by his incredible serenity and humor. Every one of his family and friends was touched by his calm resignation and remarkable faith and sense of closeness to God, knowing that his sufferings would in some way benefit others who needed special help from God.

When he finally died, his passing was peaceful, as if he were just moving into the next room. His illness and his last days were a dramatic witness to faith for all of us. His illness greatly deepened the faith and understanding of his whole family, especially his children and grandchildren.

Strangely enough, on the national news at the same time was the story of a man who had the same horrible disease. As the disease progressed, the man became depressed and then angry that he should have to suffer so much. It had no meaning, no purpose, and no belief that could help him to see otherwise. Finally, without hope, he calmly decided that the only sensible option was to end his life, which for him had no meaning. The difference between the two men was dramatic. Maybe there are some who never hear the Good Shepherd knocking at the door of their hearts, but I am sure that when they finally close their eyes and open then in their new world, it is the Good Shepherd who meets them.

Around the same time I was giving a retreat at the Dominican Retreat Center in Elkins Park, Pennsylvania. When I arrived, I stopped in the sisters' nursing-home section to visit the elderly and infirm sisters. One of them was a well-beloved nun by the name of Mother Bernadette, who had been a superior for many years. She was bedridden and felt completely useless, especially since she had been so active and productive all her life. Even with her deep faith she was finding it hard to understand any purpose to her just lying in bed day after day for endless months, now becoming years of apparent uselessness. "Would it not be better for me to be home with God, especially since I don't even suffer; I just lie here day after day, totally useless."

She then made me promise that when I went up to the retreat house I would ask the sisters to pray that God would take her home for Easter, which was just a few days off. I told her I would do that. I then left and met up with the sisters a few hours later at supper and told her of Mother Bernadette's request. Every one of them said, almost in chorus, "We will never pray for that."

"Why not?" I asked them, in total unbelief.

"Because she's our inspiration. When we get discouraged and want to throw in the towel, all we have to do is go down and sit on her bed and chat with her, and after a while, she makes our life, with its problems and difficulties, all worthwhile, and we leave with a happy and renewed spirit."

The next day I went down to see Mother Bernadette again, and she asked me if I had kept my promise. I assured her that I had. She asked me what the sisters said, and I told her they refused to pray for her death. The poor woman almost broke down crying, and mumbled, "I thought they loved me."

"That's the problem. They love you so much they can't bear to lose you. They all said: "We can't pray for that. Mother Bernadette is our inspiration. When we get discouraged and think of giving up, all we have to do is go down and visit her and after a few minutes she makes us realize that our work and all we do touches so many lives and heals so many troubled souls that we should never get discouraged. And when we leave we are completely renewed in spirit."

"Oh, thank God that I still have a purpose," the old nun replied through her tears of joy. She lived for quite a while after that, and her last days were filled with a rare kind of joy.

But not everyone finds a purpose or a happy experience in their waning days. One lady I know had recently lost her husband. They had been married for many years and had a daughter and a grand-daughter, who had been practically raised by the grandparents. When she got older, she went back to live with her mother, who had mental problems. In time, the grandfather fell ill. While he was in the hospital, the daughter and granddaughter talked him into signing a paper. Hardly a month after the funeral, the daughter visited her mother and told her that her father had signed the house over to her and that she and her daughter were moving in. She tried to convince her mother that she did it for her own good, but shortly later, after convincing the doctor that her mother was unable to care for herself, and that she could not possibly take care of her, the doctor agreed that she needed twenty-four-hour care. The daughter then committed her mother to a nursing home. "But, Father, I haven't lost my faith. Even though now I have nothing, and rarely have visitors, I feel very close to Jesus, closer now in all my sadness and broken heart, than I have ever been in my whole life. His love doesn't take away all my pain, but I have a peace knowing that my own suffering helps Jesus to save some difficult souls. You once told me that we are never closer to Jesus than when we are on the cross suffering with him. And that's just the way I feel. He is close to me, and I can't wait for him to take me home, so I can be with him and my dear husband."

I have come across many similar situations. I still can't imagine how a child could treat loving parents with such a merciless lack of compassion. Such cruelty is almost worse than murder. At least when you're dead, the pain ends.

There are other stories.

A well-loved priest, a pastor with whom I was once stationed, had worked with college students and in parishes all his life. I never met anyone who did not love and respect him. He was always cheerful, with a happy spirit, and he loved golf and playing cards with his priest friends. He just loved people. As he grew older, his sight began to grow dim. Eventually, he reached a stage where he could no longer see. In such a condition, and without any family or any living relatives, he was placed in a nursing home, where he was well cared for by the Little Sisters of the Poor. When I went to see him, I thought he might be depressed, but I was surprised to find him upbeat and happy. When I touched his shoulder, he "looked" at me and smiled. "Thank you, Joe, for coming to visit. Sit next to me so we can chat."

I sat down, and I asked him how he was and if he was well cared for.

"Yes, yes. The sisters are saints. They are so patient with me."

"You're so lovable, why wouldn't they be patient with you? I am sure they think they are caring for a saint."

"A saint! They sure know that I'm not a saint, just a cranky old man."

"You have never been that. You are still that happy spirit that everyone loves. And you still radiate peace."

"Yes, I am at peace. And even though I can't see anymore, I "see" things I never saw before. And I learn things I never knew before. It is easier to see the face of God when you're blind, and it is easier to hear the delicate voice of the Holy Spirit when you're not distracted by lots of sights. The presence of Jesus is more real than ever. He is all I have now, I so look forward to being with him. And how are you?"

"I am fine, thank God, still struggling trying to be a good priest. It's not easy."

"You are a good priest."

"I try. I have a long way to go. Pray for me."

"Give me your blessing before you leave."

"Only if you give me your blessing first."

I knelt, and he blessed me. Then I rested my hands on his head and blessed him. I kissed his bald head and hugged him and left with tears trickling down my face, his last words still sounding in my ears. I could feel a terrible sense of panic thinking what it would be like if I became blind.

The Good Shepherd was very real to that dear, lovable old priest, as he was waiting out the last few months of his life. That was the last time I saw him. He died shortly after my visit. His suffering had ended days earlier.

Epilogue

R unning through all these stories is a thread, a mystic presence in the lives of those who suffer and those who comfort them. I pray you can sense it and come to know the Good Shepherd, who promises never to leave you an orphan but to be your lifetime companion, during your sufferings as well as your good times, telling you that you are good and that all things will be well.

None of us is immune to suffering. But each of us can transcend what psychologist Eugene Kennedy called "the pain of being human." Jesus assures us, "In the world you face persecution. But take courage; I have conquered the world!" (Jn 16:33).

The Good Shepherd is with you. Moment by moment. Right now. Take courage!